Ally the Brave

Ally the Brave

Kate Dellett

ISBN: 151719881X
ISBN 13: 9781517198817

Gratitude Page

A special thank you to my mom, Linda Dellett, who has been a major supporter throughout the book writing process and has encouraged me and allowed me to pursue unlimited possibilities. I am also grateful for her unconditional love.

Thank you to my father, Brian Dellett. His fun nature, love and wisdom inspire me.

Thank you to my very motivated brother who can always find it in his heart to keep things fun.

Much gratitude to my writing coach, Lemuela Duskis, who has stretched me and taught me the wonders and magic of writing.

A huge thank you to my editors, Mary Curtis and Christina Cutting, for reviewing my book and for giving me the benefit of your insights and knowledge.

Thank you to Joe Burgess, Myrtle Dill, Renee Pawlish, Kathleen Bermea-Sullivan, Allison Cleary, Valerie Conway, Hope and Adel Johnson, Andrea Overton and Noreen Richardson for taking the time to read my book and for the thoughtful and constructive feedback. Their support through this process has been priceless.

A special thanks to Karina Usuda, Ashlyn Williams, Trevor O'Brien, Mary Darwin, Eric Dellett and Tina at Frikusha Designs for your contributions to the cover design.

Thank you to my friends. They always find a way to spice up life in the most unusual ways.

Thank you so much to Rachel Pickett for giving me such wonderful feedback and insight into the miracles of life.

Thank you to all who have touched my mind and my heart. You have impacted me and my world in an incredible way. Your contribution has been hugely important and such a gift. Thank you for giving those gifts to me in such a graceful and elegant way.

This book was written for everyone who has ever been bullied or has ever been a bully. I want you to know there is always light in your life, help is within reach and you have the power to find the light within yourself and others.

Ally would like to invite you to join the Ally the Brave community - a community committed to ending bullying worldwide.

Sign up at

allythebrave.com

and receive a free membership including a PDF for kids that introduces:
"The 3 Steps on How to End Bullying"

Table of Contents

Friends 'Til the End 1

Who Is That? 4

Billy the Bully? 7

Why and When and How? 9

Giving Back 13

Alone and Scared 16

My Lucky Day 20

What Have I Done? 23

The First Encounter 25

The Plan 28

First Attempt 31

Hello to New Friends and Goodbye to the Old? 34

Am I Done? 37

Drifting 40

Healing the Wounds 43

Friends Again? 45

Freedom at Last 49

Nails and Hair and Braiding, Oh My! 51

Fake It 'Til You Make It 55
Hippy to Drama Queen 61
Rachel's Changes 63
I Don't Care 66
Passed Over 68
The Barbies 73
The New Kid 79
Going to the Office 83
Math with Max 88
Doctor Daniel 92
It Is Him! 95
She Did It! No, He Did It! 99
Turning New Corners and Making New Friends 103
Trapped and No Way Out 107
Changes 110
Reuniting 116
Here We Go Again 122
I Can Do Better Than That 128
The Aftermath of Words Flying and Daggers Wounding 134
What Am I Supposed to Do? 138
Do You Want to Play a Game? 141
The End of the Old 146
The Start of a New Beginning 149

Chapter 1

Ally

Friends 'Til The End

*A*lly could hear the chatter of two hundred kids all talking at lunch. There was a buzz of excitement as they started to pack up their lunches.

"Everyone, stand up, empty your trash and line up for recess," said one of the teachers circling around the lunch tables.

Ally and her best friends packed their lunches into their bags, as the other kids stampeded to the door where students line up every day for recess. As Ally approached the line, she could sense the restless energy of the other kids. They were all bumping into each other trying to get to the front.

"I am so excited for recess!" shouted Jane as she spoke over the bustle. Her electric green eyes flashed with a fiery, friendly energy as she tossed her black choppy hair.

You are always excited for recess, thought Ally as she grinned at her outgoing and athletic best friend. Ally pushed her golden brown hair out of her face with a tan hand. As her hand brushed past her smooth and soft skin, a smile lit up Ally's face. Her brown eyes looked eagerly toward the cafeteria doors that would soon open for recess.

"Me, too," said a quiet voice coming from Ally's other best friend Lulu. Her blond hair framed her pale face and her baby blue eyes fluttered for a moment. As she continued to keep her slightly empty eyes on the table, her mouth slowly curved into a faraway smile. She shifted her lithe frame toward the door.

Poor Lulu, she has a hard life, thought Ally, *but even after her brother died of cancer and her father left, she had still managed to be a happy person overall, always ready with a heart-warmed smile for anyone.*

"Doesn't everyone love recess?" asked Ally as she shifted her hair out of her face again. She led her friends out the cafeteria doors onto the winding sidewalk that would take them to the playground.

"I wish, but not everyone loves it. Some people think it's a waste of time," stated Jane.

"Yes. And those will be the people sitting on the couch, watching TV while stuffing their faces with potato chips," joked Ally as she walked down the pavement, her feet skipping along the sidewalk.

Ally shot a grin at her friends as they headed to the shed that held all of the balls, jump ropes and chalk. She thought, *I am lucky to have such great friends. We're not perfect, but we're always here to support each other. We will always be the best of friends no matter what.*

The back of the shed was covered by tree limbs that stretched out from the trees planted there. Ally, Jane and Lulu went into the dimly-lit shed, which had spider webs stretched along the corners and an inch of dust on the ground.

"This place gives me the creeps," sputtered Lulu, stealing glances at the corners, "especially the spider webs!"

Duh, because you are afraid of spiders!! thought Ally as she gave Lulu a puzzled look.

Lulu shivered and her hair swayed back and forth as she fretfully reached into the ball bucket to grab a basketball.

"Ahhhhhhchhhhhoooo!!!" sneezed Lulu as she looked side to side expecting a big old hairy spider to jump right out at her.

"Bless you," said Ally as she shook her head in amusement.

"Come on, let's get out of here," stated Jane, stalking out of the shed with Lulu eagerly following her.

Before Ally followed the girls out, she took a look around the place. Her foot was almost out the door when something caught her eye. In the corner was a weird-shaped spot that was untouched by the dust and was littered with old candy wrappers.

"That's odd," Ally whispered to the darkness as strands of hair fell back in front of her face.

"Ally, come on!!" whined Jane, appearing in the doorway and interrupting Ally's thoughts.

Ally pushed the hair out of her face again.

I really need to cut my hair, Ally thought as she shook the weird moment from her head.

"Alrighty, I'm coming already," Ally said, as Jane disappeared out of the doorway with Ally jogging right behind her.

Chapter 2

Ally

Who Is That?

"Hey, are you guys ready to get beat at a game of knockout?" teased Ally as she started to edge closer to the girls.

They were dribbling the decaying balls through their legs and shooting them up to the basket. The balls bounced off the backboard and sometimes came flying back at them like boomerangs.

"Oh yeah, in your dreams!" shot back Jane, who was always ready with a quick comeback, as she picked up the ball and gripped onto it like her life depended on it. (Probably because Jane was all too used to Ally hitting the ball out of her hands. But, thankfully, for Jane's sake, Ally did not grab at it.)

"Well, we will just need to see what the score is and you will have proof that I can beat you anytime and anywhere at knockout," said Ally with a grin as she eyed the ball in Jane's arms. But Ally kept a good distance away from Jane. Anyone would stay away if they had seen the look on Jane's face that screamed *fear me*. Ally had never met anyone tougher or more competitive, and Jane's natural athletic ability had been honed through endless practice. Her parents also put a lot of pressure on her to excel at sports and insisted that she drill for hours whenever she made a mistake.

Jane continued to watch Ally with a suspicious look. Jane looked ready to jump into a volcano if it meant keeping the ball away from Ally.

"You can believe whatever you want. But, every time, you will get beat by the master of knockout," said Jane while pointing at herself. Her friendly banter covered her need to be the best, to make her parents proud. Ally was about to respond and make her move to take the ball, but Lulu jumped in first.

"When you two are done, how about we actually play knock-out or if you want to continue squawking and eyeing each other and the ball, by all means, carry on," squeaked Lulu while rolling her baby blue eyes that bounced with light from the sun.

Ally and Jane gave a look to each other that said, *you know I am just joking.* Then they gave each other a quick nod and turned to Lulu. But one of Ally's eyes stayed on the ball, and Jane kept an eye on Ally.

"Let's play some basketball!" said Lulu with excitement in her eyes.

Jane shot the ball at a perfect angle and the ball went into the net with a swish. Jane rebounded the ball and passed it to Ally. Ally squared up, extended her arm and released the ball. The ball made a perfect bank shot. They continued like this for a while until Jane missed her shot.

"Fiddlesticks!" exclaimed Jane in frustration while stomping her foot on the ground.

"It's okay," reassured Lulu in the middle of her shot. Lulu said that at the wrong time. She lost her concentration and the ball swirled around the rim and fell out of the basket.

"Oh well, maybe next time," said Lulu good-naturedly as she shrugged her shoulders as if it were nothing.

Ally smiled at her victory while saying, "Great game, guys!"

"Thanks!" they replied in unison. Then an ear-piercing whistle rang in the ears of the students.

"TIME TO LINE UP!" shouted a teacher.

Everyone in their group of friends started to walk over to the wired fence where they lined up. Every single person was huddled with their friends, chatting with each other. Only Ally saw a lonely boy wearing a bright red baseball cap walking alone, kicking pebbles with his feet.

"Who is that?" asked Ally, nodding toward the boy with the red cap.

Chapter 3

Ally

Billy the Bully?

"Oh," said Jane as her voice dropped to a whisper, "That's Billy the bully, you haven't heard of him?"

Jane was usually a quite fearless girl, but when Ally pointed to Billy, she could sense a shiver went down Jane's spine.

"No, never," replied Ally as she shook her head and glanced back at the guy.

"Well, he is in the other class and does not have any friends. Kids try to avoid him because he will bully you if you talk to him. He gets sent to the office a lot. I would hate to have him as a partner for anything," stated Jane as her voice dropped a little lower.

"Ouch. Have you ever met him?" Ally asked as she continued to study him.

Jane just shook her head "no" which sent a small burst of anger through Ally.

"Well, then why the heck are you saying these things about him?" Ally asked coolly.

Jane just shrugged her shoulders up and down.

"He looks kind of lonely and sad. I kind of feel bad for him," pointed out Ally studying him a little harder.

Jane raised her eyebrows and said, "You're kidding, right?!"

"No... But I can see that this kid is lonely, he has no friends, people avoid him and he gets sent to the office a lot. How would you feel if kids always pointed at you and avoided you?" said Ally.

"Come on, Ally! He's a bad guy! He was the one that pulled down Aiden's pants. And then he stole one of the boy's clothes in the locker room. And do you remember that time in second grade on Taco Tuesday when he took one of the tacos and smashed it in a girl's face?" she explained as she gave Ally a puzzled look.

"Okay. I understand that he did some bad things," Ally started as she received another critical look from Jane.

"Okay, maybe a lot of bad things. And I know that it's not cool to bully, but that gives us no reason to say mean things about him. I mean, how would you feel?" Ally asked as she tried to find a good way to look at this.

"Whatever," said Jane, giving Ally a confused look before turning to face the line.

Ally watched Billy slouch to his line and noticed the kids scrambling to get away from him.

Poor guy, thought Ally as she waited in line for her teacher to come. *I don't know what I would do if I did not have Lulu and Jane as friends. I can only imagine what that would feel like, let alone having no friends at all.*

Chapter 4

Ally

Why and When and How?

Ally's teacher, Ms. Nizeley, appeared and motioned the class to follow, then marched them like a parade into the building. Ally could hear her classmates' feet shuffling behind her as she followed Jane and Lulu up the stairs. As Ally entered her classroom, all of her thoughts about the lonely boy drained out of her as she took her seat and awaited instructions.

"Before we begin our read aloud, I was notified that some bullying problems were starting to surface, so today I want you all to think about how you would feel if you were being mean to someone," said Ms. Nizeley. "All of you, close your eyes and think."

Ally shut her eyes and began to think while her classmates around her did the same. *Well, I hate it when I see bullying. It makes me feel upset. And I see how hurt kids are when they are bullied. So bullying is mean.*

Then Ally's thoughts shifted to her image of Billy lining up after recess. *All of those things that Billy did sound kind of awful. But then again, why in the world would he do such things? He must be pretty upset to act that way.*

Billy looked like an angry kid, but in a way, he also looked really dejected. I wonder if he regretted those things that he did to all of those people, because I know I would if I pantsed someone in front of everyone. Sooner or later, I know I'd feel upset and disappointed with myself. I know when I say or do something mean, I end up regretting it. So other kids might feel ashamed when they pick on other people. They just might do it to feel better about themselves. Like, 'Since I feel bad about myself, you should too,' but when they bully it ends up making them feel worse.

"Now, please open your eyes. What do you think about what it feels like to be mean or to bully someone?" questioned the teacher. She scanned the room looking for hands to be raised in the air.

"Yes, Christy, what do you think people feel like when they bully someone?" asked Ms. Nizeley.

"Well, I think they feel perfectly fine when they bully someone because bullies are just plain old mean and that's all they will ever be!" Christy said confidently as she looked at Ms. Nizeley expectantly waiting for praise.

"That's one way of looking at it, but could there be more perspectives?" replied Ms. Nizeley while astonishment filled Christy's face. Ms. Nizeley looked for more hands, but apparently, everybody thought that bullies were just all mean. So Ally raised her hand.

"Yes, Ally, what is your opinion?" wondered Ms. Nizeley.

"Well, they might not feel good inside and that might be why they bully or hurt other people," Ally started off with uncertainty.

Ms. Nizeley smiled.

"Yeah. And what happens when they feel bad inside and feel upset?" asked Ms. Nizeley not daring to break eye contact with Ally.

"They keep their feelings trapped inside?" asked Ally cautiously.

"Yes, keep going," encouraged Ms. Nizeley.

"And when they feel bad and alone they take it out on others?" Ally said.

"Yes, and when they take it out on others, they…?" started Ms. Nizeley waiting for Ally to finish.

"They bully. When they bully, they push others away and the cycle continues," said Ally gaining confidence.

"Yes! There you go. Great job, Ally. So how do you think kids feel when they bully others?" Ms. Nizeley asked one more time.

Christy's face filled with envy at Ms. Nizeley's praise, but Ally just ignored her.

"I think they might feel ashamed, alone, hurt, depressed and confused, even though it looks mostly like anger and meanness when we witness it," finished Ally.

"Yes. When people bully, it is usually because they have something going on in their life and they do not know what to do about it. So when you see someone getting bullied, stand up for them, but still find compassion in your heart for the person doing the bullying. People who bully others are often lonely and have few friends and we can imagine what that would feel like," explained Ms. Nizeley looking at the entire classroom once more.

Ms. Nizeley let her words sink into the class for a couple of seconds.

"Now please come to the carpet for read aloud," she said suddenly.

Ally pushed her chair in and walked to the carpet. While her teacher read, Ally's mind began to ponder. *Is this why the kid in the red hat bullied others? I wonder what made him feel bad inside himself.* Ally's thoughts kept wandering until…

RRRIIINNNGGG!!! School was over! Finally! Ally raced to get her things; she stuffed her jacket, lunchbox, folder and water bottle into her backpack. Then she ran to the exit and took off.

Chapter 5

Ally
Giving Back

"How did you guys do on that test yesterday?" asked Lulu over the lunch table as she poked her tuna with her fork while making eye contact with Jane and Ally.

Lulu's eyes reflected the radiance of the fluorescent light above. Ally could sense the boys' stares at Lulu. She had beautiful eyes that every girl wished she had. But Ally and Jane continued to look at Lulu as if nothing were happening. Lulu did not see the boys, and Ally and Jane had no intention of mentioning it as Lulu hated to be the center of attention. Lulu turned her gaze back to decapitating her tuna.

"Not too bad, I could have done better," confessed Jane, trying to keep the conversation focused on the test.

Ally didn't say anything about the test. She had messed up, big time. She had made the simplest mistake and bombed her entire test.

"Everyone, stack your trays and line up," shouted the teacher.

Ally grabbed all of their trash and bagged it together. She watched as a big group of girls grabbed their coats and left their trays full of half-eaten food on the lunch tables.

Wow, they just expect someone else to pick up after them, thought Ally. She and her friends started to pack up their lunches.

Just then, the teacher rounded everyone up into the hallways. She started to head in after them, but the trays left on one of the tables caught her eye. The teacher looked back at the doors that led to the hallways, but no one was there. Everyone had left as soon as possible so they would not take the blame. The teacher turned to the tables and trays and started to pick up the trash. By then Ally and her friends were already dumping their trash.

"Do you want some help?" asked Ally looking at the teacher's exasperated expression. A wash of gratitude filled the teacher's face.

"Thank you so much!" exclaimed the teacher as Ally bent down to start helping.

"Here, we will help too," said Jane. She and Lulu picked up the trays.

Just then the teacher's walkie-talkie said something in a muffled voice that Ally couldn't hear.

"Would you ladies mind taking care of this while I hurry outside? A girl fell off the swing-" started the teacher.

"Of course!" interrupted Ally, "Go! We'll take care of this from here."

"Thank you!!!" the teacher said as she ran out the door and her bright neon yellow vest left the girls' view.

"Poor her," said Ally. "Always running around, picking up after us and watching 200 something kids all day. That has to be tiring."

"You said it. I would just fall apart if I had her job," agreed Jane.

"This is why it feels good that we are helping her. Kind of like giving back to the teachers that watch us," Lulu quietly replied.

Totally. Some teachers get up really early and leave the school really late just to plan and grade our work, thought Ally.

The girls finished cleaning the trays, stacked them into a neat pile and started to make their way to recess. They linked arms and walked through the doors toward the playground.

"Well, that was fun," pointed out Jane as she shook her head positively and kept on walking.

"Yeah, we should totally do that more often," replied Lulu. All the girls nodded in agreement as they turned the corner outside. The warm sun began to bake their skin as they walked out onto the blacktop. They kept a steady pace as they made their way to the playground, but suddenly they froze in their steps.

Standing before them was the lonely boy with the red cap that Ally had noticed the other day, and he was wearing a bitter expression on his face. Ally looked around to see what was happening. Crouched against a wall was a first grader looking scared to death. Ally turned back to Billy and understood. Her heart stopped beating for what felt like an eternity. But then she felt her heart begin to beat once again and take off like a race horse.

Oh no.

Chapter 6

Billy
Alone and Scared

*M*ost sane people hate school. When most kids get home from school they immediately leap into their rooms and get out their game controllers. They glue their eyes to the TV and don't come out of their games until they bleed their eyes out and even then they sometimes just keep on playing until their parents drag them away.

Well, Billy hated going home. Billy hated going home and he hated school. And he sadly didn't even have an Xbox or a PlayStation, which in his opinion made his life a lot harder.

Everyone also knows that even though you complain about your parents all of the time, you love them to pieces. Well, Billy could definitely say that neither his mom nor his dad was the lovey-dovey type. Billy hated going home because his father had the worst anger management problems.

Things were a lot better when Billy was younger. His parents rarely fought, and when they did, they would always make up the next day. Billy was rarely yelled at and the worst punishment he was given was being sent to his room. The bills were paid, stomachs were kept full and laughs abounded. Life was good.

But as Billy got older, things got worse at home. Bills started to pile up on the desk, and his parents started to fight a lot more. Sometimes they would not make up for months.

That's when Billy's father developed anger management issues. He would spend countless nights screaming at Billy's mother. His father would also shout at Billy. Sometimes it was after he made a mistake, but most of the time it was for no reason whatsoever. Billy grew a strong hatred for his father. Every time Billy saw that man, he would hear all of the insults that his father yelled at him swirling around in his head.

His mother also started to hate Billy's father. They soon got a divorce. Billy now split time between his mom's and his dad's houses.

He hated going home because even though his parents were divorced, they still fought all of the time. They used Billy as some kind of messenger, especially his father. Whenever they wanted to say something negative to each other, they would tell Billy to give the other parent the message, "Tell your mother that she's a horrible person." "Tell your father that he forgot to pay his share of your school fees again." Billy hated it. Whenever they said something mean to each other, he was left feeling horrible.

So, yes. His life did suck pretty badly.

Usually, when people get a divorce, they no longer see each other. And if they do, it is very limited. But his dad still dropped in from time to time to do a session of bellowing at his ex-wife, which sometimes lasted all night long. He also always came to Billy's school and sport events, although it seemed to Billy that sometimes he just showed up to pick a fight with Billy's mom.

Billy constantly felt like a piece of gum that was stuck on the sidewalk. In his mind, he was used, discarded and walked all over. He was in a constant mood of hopelessness.

The only people he really thought cared about him were his grandparents. They were always kind, took him for ice cream, and often told him that they loved him. But shortly after his last visit three months ago, his grandparents died tragically in a car crash. It was as if life wouldn't give him a break.

Billy loved his mother. But now that she was always at work, he felt all alone. That loneliness left him feeling like there was no way for him ever to feel like he was a part of a family again.

On top of it all, Billy was forced to go back and forth every other week between his mom's and dad's houses. Right before he left for school on Monday mornings, he had to pack up all of the stuff that he would need. Then after another dreadful day of school, he would go to whichever parent's house he was staying at, race to his room, lock the door and stay there until it was time for dinner.

That's the way it was. His parents didn't bother him, and Billy didn't bother them. The only time he had to survive listening to his parents was when one of them wanted him to give the other a message, and this usually happened on the way to school.

Going to school with all of these negative messages in his mind left Billy feeling frustrated and furious inside. He would see kids having fun, laughing and playing, and it would make him feel horrible. It made him furious. Billy bullied other kids to make himself feel better. He wanted to make people feel the same way he did, alone.

Billy was faced with a number of challenges. When he bullied other kids, it made the kids not want to hang out with him and he felt more alone. There hadn't been anyone that he really trusted to help him with his feelings since his grandparents died. With no friends, this feeling of isolation and sadness would turn into anger, which would make Billy act out and bully more. Every day, he would go to the office to have his counselor Katelyn help him sort through his feelings, but often this just made him angrier and more confused as more and more feelings started to surface.

Somewhere along the way, Billy had lost himself. He was so caught up in the cycle that he had lost touch with the sweet and caring Billy. People were afraid of him at school and his home life was a disaster. He missed his beloved grandparents, and no one wanted to be friends with him. *That is just fine*, he often told himself, even though deep inside he really wanted a friend. He really just wanted to feel loved and happy and accepted again.

Chapter 7

Billy
My Lucky Day

$\mathcal{B}$efore Billy's encounter with Ally, Jane, Lulu and the first-grader, his day had started like any other day. Billy walked down the hallway in a line with his class. He smirked at the sight of kids stepping on each other's feet trying to get a good distance away from him. Billy could see his teacher in the window's reflection shaking her head in his direction.

Great, not even my own teacher likes me, he thought as he continued to walk. Billy's heart cringed at that thought, but his face showed no sign of it at all. His class was headed to lunch and then, right after lunch, they would go to recess.

Oh, yeah, that's something to look forward to! he thought sarcastically. Billy resented recess.

I have to watch kids laughing and playing while I mope around sitting by myself, thought Billy sadly.

He sat down and started to unpack his lunch. Billy used to sit on the picnic tables outside at recess, counting the remaining minutes until the teachers called them to go inside. But now, Billy had found a hiding spot.

He would hide in the supply shed where all of the balls and jump ropes were stored. Billy would shield himself in the corner and eat candy, littering candy wrappers around him. It just pained him to see kids having a good time when he was stuck in his own world of darkness. When Billy would tire of being cooped up in the shed, he would strut around smirking at the kids and maybe even bullying some of them, and that is what he intended to do today. Billy packed up his lunch, tossed his trash and headed for the doors.

He adjusted his bright red baseball cap and walked past a group of kids, ignoring the stares as he went.

Billy looked around. The grounds frothed with bright yellow and blue colors. With swings on one side and a blacktop on the opposite side, the kids scattered across the playground and their jackets streaked it with colors like a very colorful snow blizzard as they dashed in different directions.

"Who will be the lucky winner today?" whispered Billy to himself. He scanned the playground, the blacktop and the field.

Well, the girls who play hopscotch are already scared of me, thought Billy while his heart felt a pang of sorrow.

Looks like I won't be getting a secret admirer anytime soon, Billy thought as he stopped for a second. The wind whisked in his face as he brushed his amber-brown hair out of his eyes.

Then he saw a little group of boys playing soccer. *This must be my lucky day...* thought Billy as he started to walk over.

His feet pounded the damp green grass and the sun baked his skin as he made his way over.

"Here, pass to me," said one of the boys.

"I am wide-open over here!" exclaimed another.

"Shoot the dawg gone ball!" shouted a boy.

Before the person with the ball could do anything with it, Billy sprinted over and grabbed it.

"Hey, that's ours!"

"Give it back!!"

"This is not funny," cried several of the boys at once.

Just give the ball back, Billy thought. *NO!! It's too late for that!*

"Or what will you do?" mocked Billy as he held the ball to his hip.

Billy's last comment sunk into the boys for a while…. All movement around them started to slow down. Suddenly, the cries from the playground didn't sound so loud anymore.

"Or we'll, we'll…" stuttered one of the smaller boys with short bleach blond hair, but he was cut off by the hard, ice-steel look on Billy's face.

"Or you will do what? Call your mommies? I don't think they can hear you!" shouted Billy clutching the ball even tighter.

Billy's last words drowned out the boys' cries. With the ball in his hand, Billy started to walk up the hill. As Billy walked away, a horrible feeling filled the pit of his stomach, rage started to fill his eyes and hate burned in his heart, but he kept walking up the hill with that horrible feeling bubbling inside. For a brief moment, his heart cried out, *What have I done?*

Chapter 8

Billy

What Have I Done?

Billy walked across the playground with a furious look on his face.

"What are you looking at?" Billy sneered at a group of kids who were giving him curious looks.

Billy ignored everyone's glances. He kept walking, occasionally shooting mean glances toward the other kids. Something inside spurred him to push the boundaries further. He decided to pretend to throw the ball at some fifth-grade kids who gave him a glance or even a smile.

"Ahhhh!" they screamed as they imagined the ball coming at them.

"Ha-ha. Are you going to cry? Oh mommy, the soccer ball is coming at me!" mocked Billy.

He kept the teacher in the corner of his eye each time, watching to make sure she would not catch him.

Every time Billy said something mean, it made him feel good for two seconds, but then the feeling disappeared. The horrible feeling that rumbled in his stomach only grew worse, and made his heart feel darker and darker. When Billy felt this way, he felt like he had to unleash it on kids to make himself feel better, so that's what he did.

Billy bullied just about everyone playing at recess. He would see the terror in the kids' eyes and his heart would flinch at the sight of it. It made him scared of himself for a few seconds, but he would quickly push that away. *Just look, after all that hard work, I can easily see the horror in everyone's face. Finally, I have control over something.*

Since everyone in sight had been bullied, Billy decided to walk up to the doors that led into the school. After a while, Billy saw a little kid, maybe seven years old, reading a comic book in one of the corners of the walls.

Well, I guess I get to be scary to fifth graders and first graders, thought Billy as he walked up to the corner.

"Hey, you, little baby! Why is this cute little thing out here all by himself? Did mommy forget her little handsome boy?!!" shouted Billy at the kid.

The boy looked up from his book. His face was confused as if he were unsure whether Billy was talking to him. Then the little boy stood up and his face flooded with fear and panic as if he knew what was going to happen to him.

A wicked smile filling his face, Billy walked slowly up to him. With every step that Billy took, the little boy took a step back until the first grader had his back to the wall.

All of a sudden, a small group of girls came around the corner. They were smiling, but when they saw the scene before them, their faces fell. Billy knew from the second he saw them, something was going to change.

Chapter 9

Ally

The First Encounter

Ally's thoughts crashed upon her the moment she saw Billy. At first, Ally wasn't sure what to do, but as fast as her thoughts came to her, the answers came too.

Get the first grader away from Billy.

"What are you doing?" asked Ally, trying to keep her voice steady as she stepped in front of her friends.

"And how is that any of your business?" questioned Billy snottily.

"It's my business if people are getting hurt and there is something I can do about it," leveled Ally as Billy's face filled with surprise, which made it quite clear that kids did not stand up to him very often.

Ally tilted her head slightly to Jane and Lulu and whispered, "Get the first grader away while I distract Billy; then run to the back of the shed."

Ally returned her attention to Billy and shifted her weight to her other foot as she started to walk in a circle like a wrestler, only she was trying to move Billy away from the little kid. Thankfully, Billy started to move with her.

"Well, there is nothing for you to do, so skedaddle!" exclaimed Billy as Lulu and Jane started to move toward the little kid.

Ally's friends tried to motion the first grader to come toward them. The little kid saw them doing this and moved in their direction, but he still kept his eye on Billy as he edged away.

"Why are you being so mean to this little kid?" asked Ally impatiently. Then she remembered the conversation that she had in class with Ms. Nizeley about why kids bully. Her voice softened slightly, "Did someone hurt you or is something happening in your life right now?"

Ally's words seemed to pierce him. Even though she started the conversation just to distract Billy away from her best friends, she could tell she was getting a glimpse of something else. Something was happening in his life – probably at school or at home she guessed.

"Why does that matter?" wondered Billy out loud.

"It matters because whatever is happening to you is affecting what you are doing right now," pointed out Ally.

Ally's words seemed to get under his skin. Just then, Ally saw her friends and the young boy go into the trees. Ally was about to go and join them, but something told her to stay a little longer. She continued to walk in a circle with Billy as they bantered back and forth, but she started to slow down.

"Why do you do it anyway?" repeated Ally. "I am going to take a wild guess and say that you don't have many friends. And you certainly don't make any friends when you hurt others. I am also guessing that it must not feel very awesome."

What Ally was saying was true; she could tell by looking at him. He even seemed to wonder how she knew this because he had a questioning expression on his face.

"I can see it in your eyes. You look like something has scarred you. You seem really lonely and I bet you don't have many friends," said Ally, answering the questions that were painted on Billy's face.

"Why do you bully?" Ally repeated her question. She could sense that her words were piercing his heart. She could tell she was getting through to him.

Before Ally could say anything else, Billy abruptly turned his back to her and hurriedly walked toward the school. As he walked away, Billy pondered Ally's question. Ally silently watched him, then turned and started walking toward the trees.

Chapter 10

Ally
The Plan

"What happened?" asked Jane searching Ally's eyes for answers.

"Did you get hurt?" questioned Lulu checking her arms for scratches.

"What did he say?" wondered Jane examining her for clues.

But Ally was still a little shocked by what just happened and from the look on her face, her friends understood that she hadn't had a chance to process it all.

Ally looked around and checked out her surroundings. The girls were behind the shed where all of the trees were, so a blanket of shade covered them completely. Now it was Ally's turn to look at Jane and Lulu for answers.

"Where did the boy go?" questioned Ally, starting off with the basics.

"He left. Before he left, he thanked us and told us to tell you thank you for him. We asked him what he was doing in the back of the school all alone, but he didn't say. He just grabbed his comic book and took off toward school," answered Lulu while shrugging.

All at once Ally's words from yesterday came rushing back to her. She needed to try to be nice to Billy, to find out why he bullied other kids, to try to find the real Billy underneath and maybe even to convince him to stop bullying.

"I will spare you the details, but when you guys went behind the trees, I asked him questions like, why he bullied and what he was gaining from it. I could tell my words shook him up. Like what I said yesterday in front of the class, he looked lonely and confused. You could see it in his eyes. I think we need to understand what Billy's feeling and try to help him stop bullying," said Ally.

The girls' mouths dropped open. Ally wasn't sure why their mouths dropped. Maybe it was what she had said to Billy or the thought of trying to become a friend to the biggest and meanest bully of the school.

"And why would we do this?" asked Jane.

"So we can do the right thing, do something nice for Billy," said Ally.

"But why us? Why not someone else? And what do we get from this? I don't do anything unless I benefit from it and you both know that!" exclaimed Jane.

You have no idea, thought Ally, as Lulu spoke up.

"Well, we should do it so other kids this year and next year might not have to deal with getting bullied. Other kids are too afraid to try to become friends with Billy. And Ally, as everyone knows, is brave enough to stand up to the meanest bully in fifth grade. Finally, in the future, we will not get bullied and if kids find out we helped change the meanest kid, then they will feel really grateful. Is that enough of a benefit for you, Jane?" said Lulu.

Lulu's words stunned Ally and Jane but shocked Lulu even more. She looked surprised that those last few words flew out of her mouth.

"Well then, we better come up with a game plan," said Jane, sitting down on the tall green grass.

"True. We know Billy is lonely, so he probably needs a friend. We should try to make an effort to sit with him at lunch or to walk with him out to recess and take any chance to try to be friends with him," said Ally. "Plus, we can step in if he tries to pick on someone."

"Simple enough, but we are not in the same class as him. That will make it just a little bit harder, but it's still doable," pointed out Lulu.

The girls sat silently. They tried to let it all sink in for a little while. Ally got the feeling that Jane thought becoming friends with Billy would definitely be a challenge, but it needed to be done. Lulu was right; not everyone could try to make Billy stop bullying, but that was what made it important.

Their legs started to cramp up, so they stood and started to walk to the playground hoping to enjoy the little time remaining of recess. But by the time they reached the playground, the teacher that they had helped in the lunchroom was now telling kids to start lining up. The girls moved toward the back of the line, even though the front of the line was still forming. It was as if the weight of trying to become friends with a bully was already weighing down on them. *But this has to be done*, thought Ally, *and I'm going to make sure it happens.*

Chapter 11

Ally
First Attempt

Today was their first attempt at trying to become friends with Billy. The previous day, the girls had decided that one of them would go sit with Billy at lunch. Then the following day, all of the girls would go and sit with him and try to talk with him. The girls wanted to approach Billy slowly so that way he did not feel outnumbered.

As the girls prepared to line up for lunch, they grabbed their lunch boxes and looked at each other.

"I will go sit with Billy first; you guys have a good lunch," offered Ally. She could see the worry in their faces. It only made Ally feel more intimidated.

"I will be fine," said Ally, reassuring herself as she started to scan the tables for Billy.

Her eye caught a table that only had one person sitting at it. The guy had on a bright red baseball cap and had his head bent down. The person sitting alone was Billy. Ally took a deep breath, put one foot in front of the other, and slowly approached the lonely boy. Ally sat down at the end of the table and slid to the opposite side where Billy was sitting. She began to unpack her lunch.

"What are you doing here?" asked Billy in a whisper, with his head down facing the ground while eating his sandwich.

"Why? Is it a crime to sit with you?" joked Ally.

"No, it's just that no one sits with me," stated Billy.

"True," said Ally. But she really wanted to say, *Gee, I wonder why no one wants to sit with you?*

"So, what do you like to do?" asked Ally, trying to keep the conversation going.

"What do you mean?" questioned Billy warily.

"Well, what's your favorite sport, what do you like to do at home?" asked Ally. The moment she said home, he cringed.

Okay, so something is happening at home, thought Ally, but she didn't push further. Ally knew that she was a stranger to him and it would not be wise to question about that quite yet.

"Well, I like basketball and I love chocolate," Billy replied.

"My friends and I love basketball and basically all sports," said Ally while Billy raised his face from the table.

"Really?" asked Billy.

"Totally, and who doesn't like chocolate? When I was a baby and had my first birthday, I smashed my face into my chocolate cake. I had frosting all over my face," said Ally.

"You must have looked funny," said Billy as he cracked up unexpectedly. *It's felt like forever since I've laughed,* he thought.

"I did and everyone laughed at me!" replied Ally, trying to hint that it feels better to make someone feel good than to make someone feel bad.

"Oh, by the way, I am Ally," she exclaimed smiling.

"I'm Billy," he said.

"Nice to meet you," replied Ally.

"Time to line up!" shouted the teacher.

"Can I sit here tomorrow and maybe bring friends?" asked Ally.

"Um… Sure, I guess. I'll see you tomorrow?" questioned Billy standing up with his lunch box in his hand.

"Absolutely!" said Ally. She walked away to meet up with her friends who were waiting eagerly. With a smile on her face, she thought, *I think I just made a new friend.*

Chapter 12

Ally

Hello to New Friends and

Goodbye to the Old?

Ally approached the girls.

"What in the world happened?" asked Jane.

"What did he say?" questioned Lulu.

"Was he really mean?" wondered Jane out loud.

"Not here," Ally said while directing her friends through the door that led into the hallway and then outside.

They sped outside and then went to the trees near the back of the shed, where the girls had met after they saved the first grader from Billy. The girls took a seat in the patch of grass that was still compressed from when they sat there yesterday.

"Well, what happened?" asked Jane impatiently.

"Where do I begin?" questioned Ally.

"At the beginning, of course!" exclaimed Lulu.

"Well, I sat down. I asked what he liked and what he does at home. I think something is happening at his home because he flinched when I said 'home.' He likes basketball and chocolate. He seemed surprised I sat with him but was really sweet and funny. I got the sense he has not had fun in a long time. He said I could sit with him tomorrow and bring some friends with me. So who wants to go with me?" asked Ally, while Lulu's and Jane's mouths fell open.

"Well, what were you expecting? Did you think Billy would have no interest in anything?" wondered Ally.

"We saw you at lunch laughing. Was he actually nice?" asked Lulu.

"Yes. I told him that I smashed chocolate cake on my face when I was a baby," replied Ally. "He didn't mock me when I told him. He just laughed good-naturedly."

"I didn't know you smashed your face with cake when you were little," said Jane quietly, which was unusual for her because she was usually a really loud person. Ally sensed some tension in the air.

"Is there something wrong?" asked Ally.

"Well, you looked like you were having a great time with Billy, and then you told Billy something that you have never told us, so you tell us. Is there something going on?" accused Jane.

"Wait a second, do you think that I would ditch you???" said Ally looking at the girls, expecting them to say no right away, but Jane and Lulu just looked down to the ground.

"You really think that I would ditch you!!! I have known you guys since kindergarten! And we have been best friends ever since! I would never do that! Why would you even think that??? I have only had one real conversation with Billy and that was today! It was OUR PLAN. Besides, friends are supposed to trust and support each other! I can't believe you would really think that about me, even for a second! I support you guys and trust you! Lulu, when you need help with your homework and your mom is too busy, don't I always help you? And, Jane, when you have trouble with your free throws, who helps you practice? ME!!! WHY IN THE WORLD WOULD YOU THINK THAT I WOULD DITCH YOU???" yelled Ally. She could see the shock on her friends' faces.

"Ally, we shouldn't have jumped to conclusions," stuttered Lulu, but she was cut off by Ally, who started up again.

"I don't care. I introduced you two and we all became friends from there. I just can't believe you would think this. One of us might have even been in Billy's shoes having no friends if I hadn't introduced us all!" shouted Ally.

"Well, I am done! I am tired of being a great friend and always supporting you guys, and to have you not support and trust me is hard, especially when I am trying to do something that we all agreed to do!!!" shrieked Ally. "I AM DONE!!!"

Chapter 13

Ally

Am I Done?

Ally stomped off toward the trees and ran through them. When she had run until she was out of breath, she sat down against the cool bark of a tree with her head against it. It hurt to think that her friends didn't trust her when she had known them for what seemed like forever. In the distance, she could hear the teacher shouting that it was time to line up. She heard the kids' feet pounding on the ground as they raced to the line. Ally stood up slowly and walked to the playground where she and her friends lined up every day. Ally felt the curious glances sent her way when people noticed she wasn't with her friends as usual. Ally was walking alone just like Billy was the first day she saw him.

"You all right?" asked Johnny as she fell in behind him.

"I could be better," confessed Ally.

"Is there anything I can do?" questioned Johnny.

"No, thanks for asking though," answered Ally.

Ally waited at the back of the line for her teacher to come and take her class back inside. Ms. Nizeley motioned for the class to stand up and follow her through the school. As Ally trailed behind everyone, her mood slowed her pace, like bricks were weighing her feet down. She kept a small distance between the line and herself. She approached the doors that led into the school, but before Ally could walk through them, Ms. Nizeley stepped in the way.

"Are you doing okay, Ally?" questioned Ms. Nizeley with a concerned look on her face.

"I wish. I am trying to become friends with Billy because he is lonely and has no friends. I went to go sit with him at lunch and when I came back to my friends to play with them at recess, they thought that I was ditching them and becoming friends with someone else. I realized that my friends are not supportive of me the way that I am of them. They agreed to help me with something, but then they backed out and had second thoughts," sputtered Ally.

"Well, it is nice of you to try to become friends with Billy, but what if you weren't doing that? Would your friends still try to become friends with him, if it weren't for you? It seems to me that they are being supportive just by trying to back you up when you are reaching out to Billy. They might never have even tried to become friends with Billy if not for you. They are backing you up even if they might be scared to be friends with someone who is considered a bully. And since you are becoming friends with Billy, they might feel like their friendship with you is changing. That's probably why they started to have second thoughts and backed out. Because they valued your relationship with them more than becoming friends with Billy," said Ms. Nizeley. "I know that it may be hard to understand, but you will sooner or later."

"What if I'm still mad at my friends and not able to forgive them or if I'm not ready to accept what you're saying?" asked Ally.

Ms. Nizeley simply smiled at Ally and replied, "Then take all the time you need. I know that it can sometimes be hard." Then Ally's wise teacher opened the door again and walked inside as Ally tagged along behind her.

The following day, Ally walked to lunch alone for the first time. Jane and Lulu were ahead in the line.

Ally had thought all last night about what Ms. Nizeley had said. She was right; Ally's friends had been supporting her. They were being great friends just by helping her on her quest to help Billy not be a bully anymore, but she was still annoyed with Lulu and Jane for thinking that she was ditching them. Ally knew somewhere deep inside that she was kind of overreacting but, for some reason, it still hurt to hear her friends say they thought she would ditch them.

Only an apology could heal that wound, she told herself. *And maybe I owe Jane and Lulu one, too.*

Chapter 14

Lulu

Drifting

*L*ulu had always been the quiet type. She only shared her opinion if someone asked for it.

Two years ago, her brother John, with whom she was very close, died of cancer at the age of six. The family took it very hard. Her mother cried every day and quit her job.

Lulu's father then had to take on more work, became more and more busy, and had no time to spend with his family. He woke up early each morning, left before the sun came out and then came home very late at night. He grieved alone deep inside, which made him drift even more apart from his family. The pressure of work and the depression of going to his desolate home became too much for him, so one day he packed all of his belongings and left Lulu's family. They'd never seen him since. From that day on, Lulu only had her mother and her mother only had Lulu.

Lulu's mom came up with so many excuses for her father. She said that he went to California to find work. That he was promoted and moved to Mexico. That his father got sick, so he left to go take care of him. But Lulu once heard her mother weeping to one of her friends that he was never coming back. That he had found someone else. But Lulu would never accept such a thing.

Lulu sometimes thought of her family like a glacier. The mighty and old glacier was once whole and together, but then one huge chunk and then another fell off into the sea. The ice chunks just kept on drifting and drifting away into the distance and soon were out of sight. Just like her dad and brother.

Lulu figured out that if you keep to yourself, most people do not ask questions about you. Lulu's life was written with heartbreak all over it and there was a wound deep inside of her that she believed would never heal, so she chose to close the book on that part of her life. She had never opened it since and planned never to reopen it again.

Lulu felt horrible that she had blamed Ally for planning to ditch her and Jane. Her disappointment with herself weighed her down. It felt like a car crash had happened in her stomach; it was a constant tightness in her gut that would not go away.

Ally was totally right. Ally had introduced all of the girls, and she was always there for Lulu and Jane, too. Lulu felt dreadful. She had jumped to conclusions and then she had shared them with Jane, who feared the same thing. Lulu knew she and Jane were in the wrong. They had all agreed from the beginning to make friends with Billy. When Ally and Billy started to laugh at lunch, it had just made Lulu and Jane jealous. What was even more irritating was that after lunch, Ally came over to them smiling and looking happy.

When Ally had looked like she was having a great time with Billy, it had reminded Lulu how easily Ally could adapt to people. And when Lulu thought about that, it made her remember how

Ally was offered a spot in Rachel's group earlier this school year. Rachel's group was made up of the popular girls and they wanted Ally in their group. To this day, Ally still could easily leave Jane and Lulu in the dust and become best friends with the girls in Rachel's group. Ally had always been such a kind and understanding person that a lot of people wanted to be her friend. And at times it felt like Lulu and Jane were known as Ally's friends and nothing else. Ally could do anything she wanted with her life and be friends with whomever she wanted. Lulu felt like there was always an escape door for Ally to jump through and leave Jane and her. Lulu did not want to be left behind, especially because of what had happened with her brother and father.

Chapter 15

Lulu
Healing the Wounds

That next day, Lulu and Jane walked into the lunchroom and saw Ally and Billy having lunch together. They quickly got their lunches and ran to their usual spot. Jane and Lulu believed it would be better to leave them alone.

"We really messed up," said Lulu, gloomily watching Ally eating lunch in the distance with Billy.

"You said it; things are not the same anymore," declared Jane.

"When Ally started to laugh with Billy, it reminded me of the time when Ally was offered a spot in Rachel's group, how easy it would be for Ally just to leave us and go be friends with someone else," uttered Lulu.

"But she never did," whispered Jane, which made Lulu feel worse. *Ally was right. She does support us and trust us; she just tried to do something to help someone else and we were not supportive,* Lulu thought.

Each bite of food tasted like rubber. The regret clogged her throat and made it hard to eat or even breathe. Finally, Lulu just gave up on eating and sat and stared off into space.

"Well, we have to do something to make it up to her and say sorry," muttered Jane. Apparently the regret was catching up to Jane and her eyes were starting to fill with tears.

"We can fix this," comforted Lulu, but even Lulu started to cry silently.

"You're right; we have to do this," said Jane, wiping her tears away.

"But what if we can't? What if we lose our best friend? I cannot be left behind ever again, ever!!!" cried Lulu, now crying nonstop. Thankfully, the teacher was at the other end of the cafeteria so she could not see Lulu crying her eyes out.

"Ally will never do that to us; she will forgive us. Don't worry," said Jane, as Lulu dried her eyes and wiped her red face with the back of her hand.

"Yeah, let's go! We will follow Ally out of the doors and when she stops we will show ourselves and say we are sorry and tell her we will make it up to her another time," replied Lulu as her face started to fill with color again. The two girls cleaned up their lunches and trash and walked with their heads facing down toward the floor of the lunchroom to dump their trash in the gigantic trash bin. Lulu and Jane walked out of the doors and descended into the hallways, hoping for the best outcome.

Chapter 16

Lulu

Friends Again?

The two girls without their best friend walked across the winding sidewalk. They looked around to find Ally. Lulu and Jane looked forward and could see Ally walking with Billy as they chatted about something. Lulu and Jane walked slowly behind them, but not too slowly, so they didn't look conspicuous. Then Ally waved to Billy as he walked in the opposite direction, and Billy returned her wave with a smile.

Lulu's and Jane's eyes darted to Ally as she took off toward the trees where they had had their fallout. The girls followed after her but tried to keep their distance as she disappeared into the pine trees. The girls watched Ally walk to the clearing where they met the other day. Lulu and Jane closed in after her. Jane stepped on a twig that snapped with a big pop. Ally turned around to see what caused the noise, but Lulu and Jane ducked behind a bush that was close by. The two girls watched as Ally scanned the trees and bushes around her but seeing nothing, she shrugged and carried on.

Gee, she walks fast!! thought Lulu. Lulu watched Ally come to a small tree and sit down. She leaned her back against the tree's trunk and closed her eyes. Lulu and Jane took a deep and long breath as they grabbed each other's hand. Lulu squeezed Jane's hand for reassurance as they took a big step toward the tree that Ally was leaning on. They walked slowly and tried to make Ally notice them by snapping twigs underfoot so she would not get scared or think that they were trying to startle her, but Ally's eyes remained closed. The two girls stopped when they were about four feet away from her.

"What do you want?" muttered Ally, still keeping her eyes closed.

"We came to say we're sorry," replied Jane. Lulu and Jane waited for a reply, but Ally didn't speak. Lulu moved closer to Ally and sat right across from her with Jane close behind her.

Lulu continued, "Ally, look, we are really, really sorry. When you started to laugh with Billy, it reminded us that you are smart, kind, and pretty and how you could easily leave us to join Rachel's group. You are just really good with all sorts of people, and it scared us to think that you would leave us. We were wrong. You always help me with my homework when I don't have any time or when I need help with it, and I know that you practice sports with Jane when she sometimes can't make her shots. You are a great friend, and if you ever feel like you need more help or more support, let us know because we know that we have not been the best of friends lately and you know how I hate when people ditch me-" but she was cut off by Ally.

"You guys are great friends! You are being great friends when you help me try to become friends with Billy, and you do plenty more. You do trust me and support me. I was just too angry to acknowledge it. I am so sorry. I should have never yelled. I would never leave you two for Rachel's group. Those girls are too worried about their makeup and about gossiping to ever be my best friends. You guys are and you always will be my best friends," replied Ally, finally saying what she had been thinking about saying all day. Her eyes were open wide and full of tears as she finished.

"We are so sorry. You are right; we will always be friends," said Jane while she bent down giving everyone a group hug. Lulu's eyes were flooded with tears, but she had never felt better. It felt good to know that Ally had no interest in becoming best friends with Rachel's group and that Ally was never going to abandon her. Lulu always kept a wall up between herself and her friends, but once Ally said that she would never leave her, the wall fell down like it was just waiting for a reason to fall. All three friends broke out into tears as they hugged each other. They let go and started to wipe the tears from their relieved faces.

"I can't tell you how boring it was to sit with Jane alone at lunch," joked Lulu, suddenly feeling bolder than she had ever felt before.

"I was feeling crushed about having to sit with you for an entire lunch," shot back Jane as a grin spread across her face.

"Like you said, you must have been blurred out from the world because I was like total coolness. Some people even came to sit with us and listen to me tell about amazing me, but they left because Jane, the 'totally sad and depressed' girl, drove them off," joked Lulu in a high-pitched girly voice that made her sound so ridiculous it made Ally and Jane crack up.

Lulu felt more alive than she had felt in a long time. She felt like she could joke about things much more now. All Lulu wanted to do now was make people laugh, and when she did, it made her feel good inside.

The whistle that the girls had heard for the past five and a half years rang once more and all the students raced to the wired fence. Even though everyone else was running, the girls locked arms and slowly walked over to the playground. The girls felt so much better, like a weight had been lifted from their shoulders. Their pace was unhurried while they tried to savor what had just happened. Only two things ran through Lulu's mind.

Ally is my friend again.

Ally is not going to leave me behind.

Chapter 17

Lulu

Freedom at Last

Lulu finally figured out why she hated when people got ahead of her in life, such as when a friend skipped to the next grade in school or if people changed groups to be with new friends or any time that someone left her. Lulu hated it when someone left because that is what her father had done to her.

During the conversation in the trees with Ally and Jane, Lulu, without meaning to, had opened the book she had closed two years ago. In her mind, she had flipped through the pages of her past during their conversation. While she did this, she felt her sadness, her sorrow, and all the feelings that were a part of herself. It felt like she was reliving the past, but it felt good to see that she could let go of the horrible things that had happened to her a long time ago. Lulu had seen that her past did not control who she was; she controlled that. She could choose to be the unhappy, lonely kid in the back of the class or the loud, outgoing kid that keeps others entertained at lunch. Each of us can choose who we want to be in the world.

Lulu knew that her father didn't leave for his job or her grandfather. She did not know exactly why he had left her and her mother. But she knew now that she did not need to constantly carry that fear around with her.

She noticed that when her father had left her, she had felt devastated. And as time went on, she remained devastated even though she had her mother, her friends and a good life. She now realized that her fear of abandonment held her back. Lulu could finally let go of some of that pain and appreciate her relationship with her mom and her friends.

Lulu had kept that sorrow inside of her and had chosen to be the quiet and shy kid, but now she wanted to be something different. She didn't want the world to see her as the depressed kid that held on to things that had happened in the past. She wanted to be the free person that was happy and secure.

Understanding that she might never be able to forgive her father, Lulu also acknowledged that she could accept her fear of being abandoned and learn to let it go. It was only a small part of life, but as time went by, she knew that she would be able to let it float away without her. She felt like a new person – much lighter, happier and freer.

Chapter 18

Jane

Nails and Hair and Braiding, Oh My!

Jane was loud and proud. She was proud of her athletic skills, of which her mother and father were also proud. Jane was never afraid to speak her mind or share her opinion. But Jane's parents pushed her to excel in sports. They cared less about how well she was doing in school; they just wanted to know that their daughter could shoot a penalty kick and that she was the best player on her team. Her parents always came to her practices and made sure she could execute each move flawlessly. If she messed up on a shot, even if it barely missed the goal, her parents would take her home and make her stand outside and shoot on her goal until she could make 20 shots in a row. Her parents made her practice for what seemed like forever, even if it was freezing outside or snowing.

When Jane got home from school, her parents made her do her homework. When she was done, she had to march outside and practice at whatever sport her parents wanted her to do better.

Of course, Jane wanted to please her parents very much, and when she couldn't do it, it made her feel like she was a loser and a failure. Jane hated that feeling more than anything else in the world. She could handle it when mosquitoes bit her and when she got kicked in the shin playing soccer, but she couldn't stand feeling like she let down her family.

It feels good to be forgiven, thought Jane as she sat down on the rocky pavement. Ally had just forgiven Lulu and Jane for thinking that Ally would ditch them for Rachel's group or Billy, and speaking of Rachel's group, Jane watched Rachel and the rest of her gang walk up to where Ally, Jane and Lulu were sitting.

"Like, what's up, girlfriend?" asked Rachel in a girly voice, as Jane watched Lulu make a sour face.

"Nothing. How was your recess?" questioned Ally as Jane and Lulu tried to hold back giggles.

"It totally could have been better. There was, like, no gossip today except that Brian has a crush on Linda and, like, that is totally old news, so boring. We only got to sit around and there was nothing to talk about," answered Rachel.

"Next time that happens, you could come and play basketball with us," suggested Jane while Rachel turned to Jane with a shocked and slightly disgusted face.

"You mean sweat? NO!!! I just got my hair done by a professional hairstylist and even when my hair isn't looking as glamorous, my nails are done! Are you crazy? I will never play basketball!" exclaimed Rachel. Then Rachel turned her face toward Ally and her expression calmed down immediately.

"So do you want to totally, like, come hang out with us? We could, like, braid each other's hair, and I brought nail polish, so we could totally have so much fun," said Rachel to Ally.

Right after Rachel said it, Ally answered with a smirk on her face, "No thanks, I would rather play sweaty basketball."

Rachel looked like she just took an arrow to her heart. "Well, forget it, I guess you just aren't cool enough to do it anyway!" exclaimed Rachel.

"I really don't care that I am not cool enough to wear pink nail polish," replied Ally coolly, as if she were not making fun of her but just sharing her opinion in the nicest way. At this point, Lulu and Jane fell to the ground laughing.

"Oh, and by the way, it's totally not cool to give mean glances and act like you are better than others or to exclude them from whatever," said Ally in a high-pitched girly voice.

"Well, I don't care; you have no personality to ever be my friend," said Rachel matter-of-factly.

"Well, you never fit the description of my best friend either, sweetheart, so it looks like we both win," replied Ally in a western voice. By this time, Jane and Lulu were howling with laughter.

"Come on, girls; let's go spend our time with classier people," replied Rachel. She turned with a flip of her hair and walked away from Jane and her friends.

"It was nice talking to you, too!" shouted Ally as Rachel's group stalked away.

"That was so funny," said Jane.

"You mean sweat??? NO!!!" mimicked Lulu in Rachel's voice.

"Hey, thanks for not going with them," said Jane.

"No problem, I would never become best friends with them. There is nothing wrong with liking that stuff, but it is not my style," replied Ally.

"Totally, I could never see you wearing makeup or getting excited about braiding someone's hair," pointed out Lulu.

"No way, I would rather do just about anything other than wear makeup," agreed Ally as the entire class stood up to follow their teacher into the building.

"I really can't see any of us wearing makeup in fifth grade unless we were forced to," said Ally.

"Well, I would put up a real fight," replied Jane.

"Me too. And if they fought me, they wouldn't stand a chance," teased Lulu. Jane liked the new Lulu who was starting to surface. She seemed free and not so shy.

"The only way you would survive that was if you were with me. I would give them a right and a left," said Jane, shaking her fists in the air.

"You both are forgetting one very important thing," said Ally, coming into the conversation. Jane and Lulu turned their heads toward Ally.

"Yeah, what's that?" questioned Lulu.

"The most important part...me!! I would swoop down on a vine, kick all of the bad guys in the face, scoop up you two and bring you to safety," exclaimed Ally. The girls laughed like crazy until they got into the building.

Chapter 19

Jane

Fake It 'Til You Make It

The entire class filed into the classroom where Ms. Nizeley was waiting for them. It might just have been Jane's imagination, but did she just see Ms. Nizeley wink at Ally when she came in? Jane shrugged and took a seat at her desk. She could be a mysterious teacher at times, but Ms. Nizeley was caring and kind, so everyone in the class loved her.

"Did you all have a good lunch?" asked Ms. Nizeley.

"Yes," chorused the class.

"Excellent, so today we are going to do something different. Today we're joining the other fifth-grade class. The teachers are going to pair you up with someone from the other class and you will just talk about yourself, your family or anything else. Try to be open with each other and listen. You might even make a new friend."

Did her teacher just wink at her? Jane gave a questioning look at Ms. Nizeley, but she only smiled at Jane.

That was weird, thought Jane as she pushed in her chair and joined Ally and Lulu in the line.

"I wonder who I will be partnered with?" mused Lulu out loud.

"I hope it is someone nice," stated Ally.

"I wonder why she is making us do this; does she want us to make friends with the other class?" asked Jane.

"Maybe it is just a fun activity," suggested Lulu.

"Maybe," said Jane, not totally convinced. She had the feeling that it was a little more than that.

Ms. Nizeley's class filed into Ms. Brown's classroom. All of Ms. Brown's students were sitting at their desks, so Ms. Nizeley's class took a seat on the carpet.

"Hello, so Ms. Nizeley may have told you all, but a student from Ms. Nizeley's class and a student from my class are going to be partnered up. We just want you to talk about yourselves and have fun," stated Ms. Brown.

"Any questions?" Ms. Brown asked as she looked around for hands in the air. "No? Great. Ms. Nizeley is going to read the names of your partners off the list," said Ms. Brown as Ms. Nizeley grabbed a clipboard with pieces of paper on it.

"Janet and Kirstyn, Brenna and Alex, Eric and Dyllan, Lulu and Emerson, Caroline and Savanna, Dom and Mary, Ally and Billy, Jane and Rachel."

Wait, what??? I am partners with Rachel??? Jane thought in shock. *Well, Ally got Billy so she must be happy.*

Ms. Nizeley called out more names, but Jane did not listen. Lulu got Emerson. Emerson was pretty nice; at least she didn't get Rachel.

To Jane, Rachel was like a Barbie doll. She had perfect sun-streaked blond hair and always talked in a high-pitched voice, just like a Barbie doll.

"Everyone, settle down!" shouted Ms. Brown. Jane hadn't noticed that everyone was sharing with their friends about their partners, so Jane turned to Lulu.

"Man, I feel so bad for you; you are paired with Rachel," said Lulu to Jane as Ally walked over to them.

"A bummer, right? The only thing she is going to talk about is hair and how perfect her nails are. I will be talking about how you can easily shoot a jump shot if you square up right," replied Jane as Ally started to catch on to the topic.

"Well, I'm with Billy; I get to talk with him some more," said Ally, with a hint of excitement in her eyes.

Well, easy for you to say! You know him; think about what if another person was paired up with him. They would be too scared to say anything!!! thought Jane.

"Now, everyone, please find your partner," exclaimed Ms. Nizeley over the commotion.

"Wish me luck," said Jane. She turned and looked for Rachel. Jane found Rachel standing with her gang of makeup lovers over near their desks.

"Rachel, come on," whined Jane.

"Oh, I switched partners with Cassidy; you are now partners with Kevin," said Rachel, not even looking at her as her finger pointed to a guy who Jane guessed was Kevin.

"As much as not being partners with a girl who is in love with herself sounds fantastic, rules are rules and you are my partner, so deal with it," replied Jane coolly, and as Jane predicted, her statement got Rachel's attention.

"Excuse me, I have to go deal with someone who believes that beauty is a crime," muttered Rachel to her friends as she turned and slowly walked over to Jane.

"Now look, I am not happy with this arrangement either, but we have to do it. You only have to talk to me for 20 minutes and then I can go back to my friends who have an actual interest in life," exclaimed Jane, as Rachel rolled her eyes.

"What do you like to do at home?" asked Jane trying to start a conversation.

"I LOVE to paint my nails," she exclaimed joyfully.

"And..." Jane pushed as she rolled her eyes.

"Well... I like to ride my bike," answered Rachel.

Oh, so the Barbie does do something that falls under the category of exercise, thought Jane.

"Really, have you ever ridden a trail in the mountains?" questioned Jane, very surprised.

"Plenty of times, I ride my bike a lot," replied Rachel.

"I have ridden a lot too, so that is something we have in common," said Jane.

"Yeah," agreed Rachel.

"But I thought you hated anything that involved sweating," exclaimed Jane, confused.

"That is me with my friends," she said quickly.

"Well, who are you without your friends?" Jane asked slowly, not quite sure where this conversation was going.

"What I mean is that the person you saw earlier was the girl that I am with my friends," Rachel replied even more quickly.

After she had spoken, a small silence settled over them.

"Who are you without your friends?" Jane asked again quietly trying to meet Rachel's eyes, which were now glued to the floor.

"You are not going to let this go, are you?" she asked, returning a question with a question.

"Well, look at that; you know what? You know me better already," Jane joked trying to fill the uneasy feeling.

Rachel laughed and raised her eyes up to meet Jane's.

"Fine, I used to wear earthy colors and liked to be around nature, but last year my friends all started to wear makeup and always gossiped about others. One of them told me, 'In order to fit in, you have to become a girly girl,' so I lost the earthy look and became the 'I don't want to chip my nails' girl," replied Rachel.

"You shouldn't put a mask over yourself, sometimes it's best to show the real you that is underneath," said Jane.

Rachel just shrugged.

"It is just easier this way. I don't get into a huge fight and everyone stays happy," said Rachel with a touch of grief.

"Everyone but you," muttered Jane quietly.

"Well, if I came to school like I used to, my friends would totally ditch me and then who would I hang out with?" questioned Rachel.

"Hey," said Jane, grabbing her hand and looking into Rachel's eyes.

"You can always come and hang out with me and my friends and my offer will always stand," said Jane. Rachel's eyes filled with a tad bit of hopefulness, but then the hopefulness was drowned by doubt.

"But, of course, you are probably going to have to sweat, so..." Jane joked.

"Wow. Thanks for reminding me about this morning," Rachel laughed as she swept strands of blond hair out of her face.

"And thanks, I will think about it," added Rachel.

Jane dropped Rachel's hand and gave her a smile.

"Everyone, please thank your partners and would Ms. Nizeley's class please line up?" shouted Ms. Brown over everyone's voices.

"Well, see ya," said Rachel as she started to walk over to the place where she and her friends were sitting earlier.

"Hey, by the way, it sounds like I would like the earthy and nice Rachel way better than the 'I want perfect hair' Rachel," added Jane as the kids all started to talk loudly. Rachel just gave Jane a smile and a wave and continued to walk to where her friends were motioning her over.

I would hate that, never being able to be myself, thought Jane. She walked to where Lulu and Ally stood.

"How was it?" Jane asked.

Chapter 20

Jane

Hippy to Drama Queen

"Well, Emerson just talked about how he is very strong and how he is so smart and talented," said Lulu.

"Well then, you guys must have talked about absolutely nothing this entire time," Jane joked as her friends broke into a round of giggles.

"Billy and I just talked about how the Broncos failed last night," Ally said.

Jane got the feeling that there was more that Ally was not telling them, but she pushed that thought out of her mind.

"Apparently, Rachel is not the stuck up girl we thought she was," exclaimed Jane as she and her classmates started to walk out of Ms. Brown's room.

"What?" Lulu and Ally both cried in absolute shock.

"The only reason she likes nail polish and perfect hair is because her friends like it," Jane said, answering Lulu's and Ally's questioning looks.

"What? Her friends are like peer pressuring her?" Lulu asked trying to clarify Jane's statement.

Jane nodded while Lulu shook her head.

"That is so sad," whispered Lulu, keeping her voice low because they were in the hallway.

"I feel kind of bad for her," confessed Ally.

"Well, I said if she ever gets into a fight with her friends because she gets tired of acting like a drama queen, then she can come and hang out with us," retold Jane.

"I would have said the same thing," agreed Lulu.

"Well, maybe that will happen to her one day, and if it does, we will be there to support her," said Ally as they walked into their classroom.

Chapter 21

Jane

Rachel's Changes

"Ugh!!! I am so tired of school!" Lulu cried to Ally and Jane as they met at the flagpole the next morning. Ally just laughed in reply as Jane smiled.

"Everyone is tired of school, Lulu. What makes you so different?" Ally teased as they walked near the playground.

"One reason. It's me we are talking about not just some person off the streets!" Lulu exclaimed as she threw her hands up in the air.

"Wow," Jane laughed as Ally shook her head.

"I still don't understand what the heck is wrong with you!" a voice yelled from around the corner.

"Calm down. You are just overreacting!" someone shouted back.

Oh, drat. This cannot be good, Jane thought as she looked at her friends for some answers. Ally put a finger to her lips to shush Jane and Lulu as she started to slowly descend into the forest. Jane and

Lulu followed her footsteps and ducked behind an outcropping of trees. They came to a stop and peeked their heads around the trees.

Jane saw a blond girl wearing a pink sweater and jeans. Jane squinted at her and could see no traces of makeup - no lipstick, no foundation, no eye shadow, no nothing. Jane could actually see Rachel.

She could also see another girl. She was wearing burnt red eye shadow and had her hands on her hips. She had heavy red lipstick and looked over at Rachel with an uncompromising and judgmental look.

"Oh my gosh, Rachel! Get yourself together! I have some extra makeup in my locker that you can use so you don't embarrass yourself in front of everyone," she tried to reason as she gestured and turned to go back toward the school.

Rachel stood still for a moment and locked her eyes onto her friend Jessica like she wanted to go with her. But then her eyes drifted to the ground and she whispered, "No."

Jessica wheeled around and her expression darkened even more as she placed her hands on her hips.

"What do you mean no?"

"I mean no. I am done doing this. I am not wearing a mask anymore. I will not cover my mistakes with makeup anymore. You cannot fix everything with makeup. You can't hide who you really are! Jessica, don't you see? I am tired of this and it looks like you might be too," she stated in almost a whisper as she slowly looked up at Jessica.

Jane watched Jessica sweep over Rachel's face for some kind of a clue. But then her face just hardened again and she shook her head.

"No, Rachel. We are in fifth grade. It is time to grow up and accept life's challenges. The only way that we are able to do that is to fit in," Jessica claimed as she flipped her hair out of her face.

Rachel didn't say anything in response. She just shook her head and looked down at the ground again.

"I am going to go hang out with my girlfriends. You know my locker combination. You can use any of the makeup inside of there. I honestly hope that you will," Jessica restated as she clomped her stylish wedges on the ground and stormed off past Rachel.

Rachel didn't even turn to watch her walk away. She just stood in place. Finally, she turned toward the school and walked across the playground blacktop.

Chapter 22

Jane
I Don't Care

The following week Jane, Ally and Lulu sat together at the tables eating lunch in the cafeteria. Billy had been home sick with the flu on Friday and Monday and was still out sick today, so Jane and Lulu still hadn't had a chance to have lunch with him. Jane was super happy that the three girls were all friends again. Even though each of them might have had a few scars from their fight, everyone was still pretty happy.

"Hey, did you guys hear about Rachel the other day?" Lulu asked as she took a drink from her juice box.

"Which part? That she wore her hair down on Monday and had no perfume on her for an ENTIRE day!" Jane asked emphasizing the word "entire" quite a bit.

"I heard the same thing! I also heard that she invited her friends for a bike ride on Friday! And that she did not wear nail polish on Monday! What an absolute shocker!" Ally reported, jumping into the conversation with a big smile on her face.

"I am so proud of that girl!" Jane exclaimed happily as she bit into her pizza.

"I am glad she is taking a new turn in her personal appearance," Lulu declared.

"Me too. I mean, she looked pretty unhappy the other day when we 'spied' on her. But now she sounds pretty confident in her decision!" Ally stated with a smile.

"We did not spy!" Jane called out as she giggled.

"No. We just hid behind a tree and eavesdropped," Ally said matter-of-factly.

"Yes, but 'eavesdropped' is such a strong word. Why don't we call it casually listened?" Lulu teased as she playfully shoved Jane.

"I like that word choice a lot better," Jane admitted.

"Well, I don't care!" shouted a voice.

"You don't care about what?" Jane asked the girls.

"I didn't say anything," replied both girls in unison.

Jane's head swiveled around to view the scene across the table behind them, and Ally's and Lulu's heads followed suit. Jane could see a small group of girls standing in front of the table giving the girl across the table an icy look. Jane took a better look at the girl. *Oh my gosh! That's Rachel!!* thought Jane.

Rachel was wearing a light blue shirt that had a peace sign on it and green shorts. Jane could barely recognize Rachel. She didn't have on makeup, a scarf or any jewelry at all.

"Like, wow! What happened?" said Lulu in astonishment with her mouth open.

Chapter 23

Jane
Passed Over

"I barely recognize her," Ally agreed, looking over at Rachel, and continued, "What is she doing?"

"I don't care if I look like a hippy; this is me!" exclaimed Rachel. "Everyone else in the group hates the girly look. The only reason everyone wears makeup is to fit in and to look older – like a cool sixth or seventh grader. They hate wearing makeup and the smell of hairspray! Even you hate it, Jessica. You used to wear the color yellow and it was your favorite! Who cares if no one else likes it? It only matters that you like it! And I know that everyone in our group of friends actually hates the color pink and makeup and girly things! Yet, everyone wears it! And why would that be? To fit in? Well, guess what, people? The future is calling and it said that no one cares what you wore when you were in fifth grade! They care if you were nice and if you were a person that people could count on! And none of us are that!!! So why do we put on this act that we love being girly?" shouted Rachel.

By now everyone in the lunch room was staring at Rachel, except for the teacher who was busy fussing with a fifth-grade boy because the only thing he was eating was a fruit roll-up for lunch.

"Rachel, I know that you had a hard day yesterday, so how about we go and sit down and discuss this quietly?" asked one of the girls who was friends with Rachel. She had a crazy complicated looking updo and her finger nails were painted purple and she had matching purple mascara.

"No, Lacey. That is not the way this is going to work," said Rachel. "It is time to accept the past and move on to the future, and for all of us to really be ourselves. Someday, you all will look back on this day and what will you see? You being stuck in your old way of thinking or you choosing to be yourself?" finished Rachel with such grace and wisdom.

"Well, we have had it with you too, always making us feel like we are never good enough. We have put up with you and your expectations for a long time, so why this sudden change of heart?" asked Jessica, who looked angry and confused.

"When have I ever made you feel like that? You were the one who decided we had to be a certain way! And even if I did make you feel not good enough, guess what? I'm sorry. No one is perfect! We are human and humans make mistakes," Rachel exclaimed throwing her arms up into the air. "I can't live in the shadows anymore. I won't be something I am not."

"We don't like this Rachel. We want the old Rachel back. What the heck is wrong with you?!" countered Jessica.

"If you guys can't accept me as I am, then I am done," shouted Rachel, turning quickly to walk away.

"Don't you turn your back on us!!!" screamed Jessica.

"Well, you did that to me a long time ago," said Rachel.

She turned her back on the girls she had once called friends and started to walk through the aisles of lunch tables.

Sometimes, when you think you know a person, you don't really know them at all. Everyone knew the girly-girl Rachel and left her at that. But no one ever took the time to really see her. She was always just passed over as the drama queen. But now, Rachel had changed into a totally different person. And the world (at least her social group) was not quite ready for it. So they turned on her.

What shocked Jane and her friends more was that Rachel walked all the way down to their table and plopped herself right next to Jane.

"Hey," muttered Rachel to the girls as they tried to wipe the traces of shock off their faces. Rachel nervously started to twirl her hair and stared at the table.

"So, how's your day been going?" asked Lulu with a stunned stare.

"Wow, nice opening topic. But, if you must know, not too hot. But you guys probably already heard," replied Rachel in a whisper.

"It's not like you just had a fight with your friends in front of the entire cafeteria," Ally whispered to herself quietly.

"You were really confident though, and I was amazed at how you handled it with such grace," comforted Jane, secretly amused.

"Thank you; I was actually shaking though," confessed Rachel with a look of gratitude on her face for the words that Jane had just spoken.

"Couldn't tell," shrugged Ally as she took a bite out of a potato chip.

"Thanks. I was really scared and I still am," she admitted as she continued to twirl her hair.

"Do you think the teachers heard you?" Ally wondered.

"Probably not," Jane chimed in.

"Wow. I totally did not think this through. What will my friends think? Who will I sit with during lunch?" wondered Rachel out loud.

"Calm down. First of all, who cares what your friends think? You said it yourself, thirty-something seconds ago. And like I said before, you are going to sit with us as long as you need. And you did nothing wrong! You simply spoke your mind!" Jane exclaimed as she took a drink of her juice.

"It's just like you said, who cares what other people think? And you can sit and hang out with us for as long as you like," answered Lulu.

"Really?" asked Rachel with a hopeful look on her face.

"Of course, we are going to play basketball at recess today; do you want to play with us?" said Ally, as her eyes jumped from Rachel to Jane and next to Lulu, looking unsure. It was just the other day that Rachel had said she hated doing anything that involved sweating.

"Totally, I love basketball, but I like to bike more than play basketball," answered Rachel truthfully.

"What else do you like to do?" asked Lulu curiously.

"Well, I love to play soccer. My favorite color is blue, not pink by the way, and I love to be outside," responded Rachel.

"That sounds like Jane; she hates the color pink and loves to play soccer," compared Ally as Jane gave Rachel a warm smile.

"But I play all sports," corrected Jane as she smiled at Ally.

"Yeah, and you are totally great at all sports!" exclaimed Lulu.

"Line up and clean up your trash!" hollered the same teacher that the girls helped clean off the tables last week.

"Come on," said Ally to the girls, "let's clean up our trash."

The group of four girls cleaned up and jumped in line to go outside.

Chapter 24

Jane

The Barbies

"How's it going, hippy?" asked one of the girls whose name was Lacey.

Anger bubbled up inside of Jane. Rachel was really nice and those girls had no right to pick on her.

"Don't listen to the Barbies," whispered Jane to Rachel. Rachel giggled. Lacey seemed oblivious to what Jane had said. She gave the girls a hard look and walked out the doors.

"Is that what you call us behind our backs?'" Rachel asked.

"What? You mean little old us? Why, we would never say such a thing!" Ally said sarcastically. Rachel just fell into a fit of giggles.

"Yeah. But seriously, don't listen to them. They just can't face the truth about what you said today," comforted Ally while laughing inside about Jane calling Lacey and her group Barbies.

"You are right, but they are still my friends. They used to be so much more kind and real. Lacey has always loved animals and she even has a puppy at her house. But now she barely mentions animals at all. Abby has always loved art, but now she pretends to hate art class. They used to be nice and trustworthy. I miss them, even if they are not being who they really are," said Rachel sadly. Jane put her arm around Rachel's back to comfort her.

"Don't worry; you will be fine. That is completely normal. Everyone misses someone after they have a fight," chimed in Lulu.

"I know, but I feel like a part of me is missing without them," muttered Rachel.

"Just because your friends are angry with you and being jerks does not mean you have to be upset. Whether they know it or not, their anger is caused by their thoughts and fears about themselves. It really has very little or nothing to do with you even though they are trying to put the blame on you. And sorry about saying they are being jerks, but in this moment it's true," said Ally defensively.

"What?" started Lulu with a puzzled look on her face. "What do you mean, Ally?"

"Well, it's just that the words we say to others and the way we treat them is really just a reflection of what is going on in our own lives or of our own insecurities and what we believe in some way about ourselves. When Jessica gets mad at Rachel for not looking or acting a certain way, it's really Jessica's fear of not fitting in. It's kind of like a boomerang. When people get mad or say things about us, it's really about them and what they are thinking and believing about themselves. And when we get mad or say things about others, it's really about us," explained Ally.

"I know for me, when I get upset with you guys, it's really more about how I'm feeling about myself. Even last week when I was upset with you and Jane for not trusting me I actually wasn't trusting YOU in that moment. I wasn't trusting you to work through your own thoughts and still be my friend. Sometimes it just takes me a while to look at the thoughts I'm believing and figure it out," finished Ally with an impish smile.

Ally's words crashed onto Jane like a giant wave. Jane could totally relate. Just because someone got angry and upset with you, it didn't mean you also had to get angry and upset or take it personally. When Jane's parents got frustrated with the way she was playing soccer or any sport, it made her feel less than good enough. Just because her parents got upset, it didn't mean that Jane had to as well. At that moment, Jane realized that the anger and frustration belonged to her parents and that she could choose to take it on or not. Her face and body froze as this realization sunk in.

"Is something wrong?" asked Lulu with a hint of concern in her voice. Jane realized that she had shock painted all over her face.

"Um, nope," stuttered Jane as the girls stopped and stared at her. Jane forced her face to return to normal and then she put on a smile.

"I just remembered that I, uh, forgot to bring in my homework," lied Jane.

Just then someone called out, "Hey, Rachel!" and the girls turned their heads toward the noise.

"Who was that?" asked Ally.

"Guess what your new nickname is? Hippy! I guess you are not cool enough to be with the cool group," taunted Jessica as she crossed her arms.

"Oh great, not her again!" whispered Rachel, so that Jessica and her posse could not hear.

"What do you mean? She is hanging out with us!" stated Jane. Jessica gave Jane a disgusted look.

"Aww! You know what, honey, keep on believing that. I won't be the one to crush your dreams," Jessica answered snottily. "Rachel could have, like, totally been popular, but she threw her life away!"

"So what exactly is not popular? The color blue? Animals? Art?" asked Rachel, as Lacey cringed at the word 'animals' and Jessica cringed at the word 'art.' Lacey and Jessica didn't even dare to defend what they cared for.

"Your definition of popular is different from everyone else's. Others only care if you are nice and considerate, not if you like the color pink and you have perfect hair," said Rachel.

"Yes, they do!" argued Jessica as she stomped her foot like a two-year-old. As Jessica fought for her group, some of her posse were starting to lose focus and interest.

"Name one person," dared Ally.

"Well, there is…there is-" stuttered Jessica, clearly unable to name anyone who cared.

"I thought so. No one cares, so why do you?" asked Rachel. Jane, Lulu and Ally only had to sit back and support Rachel. Rachel was independent.

The girls were like a building and Rachel only needed a base. And once Rachel had a base, she could keep going until she touched the sky. Plus this was Rachel's fight. The girls didn't want to get caught up in the drama, but if Rachel needed some help, the three best friends would be there.

"Well, never mind, the point is you lost your coolness. Now you can hang out with THESE people," said Jessica rudely as she pointed to where Ally, Lulu and Jane were standing.

"They like to play sports! And sweat and RUN! That's right, I said "run." This is so not like you!" cried Jessica. She was starting to lose her reasons to be someone she was not. Her face began to turn pink. Jessica's group of girls finally lost interest in this conversation and headed toward the playground.

"Ally, Lulu and Jane are nice. They don't pretend to be someone they're not. They actually care! They care if I am hurting;

they care if there is something happening at home! They are like a pack of wolves. No one gets left behind," stated Rachel.

The girls were just outside the school building and they could hear kids screaming with delight as they climbed the rock wall and slid down the slides. The girls sat in silence as they listened to the fifth graders running around. What Rachel had said was sinking into Jessica, who was clearly the group leader now. Jessica held her head high as she looked down on Rachel and her new friends.

Jessica and Rachel had been close friends before the fight. It was clear that both of them still cared deeply for one another, despite their angry words. At this point, the rest of the girls had left and gone to the playground. Still feeling defensive, Rachel started picking at Jessica, knowing right where to hit her with her words.

"You of all people should know how it feels to not be heard," Rachel declared, knowing how Jessica's parents always focused on her brother.

"Don't you dare talk about Matthew!" cried Jessica with pain drowning her face as her cheeks turned red.

"Why? Because you are embarrassed? Is that why you are always trying to change yourself and others?" asked Rachel as her voice died down a little.

"Who is Matthew?" asked Jane in a whisper to Ally and Lulu.

"No idea," replied Ally as Lulu shrugged her shoulders. They had the same questioning looks on their faces as Jane did.

"Just because you want to be perfect does not mean everyone else does," said Rachel in almost a whisper.

"I just hate it! I hate how I come home and my parents only care about him. They'll ask me, 'How was your day, sweetheart?' and tell me, 'I love you,' but they never really listen to me," Jessica screeched as she went to cover her face with her hands.

"Can't they see I am just as important as Matthew? I am even the first born! When I try to talk to them, Matthew will need something and then they just leave me! I hate it! And when I try to draw attention to myself, they don't even realize I'm there. If I ever got a tattoo, I don't think they would even notice!" bawled Jessica as she started to cry.

"I think Matthew is her younger brother," whispered Jane to Lulu and Ally.

"I am so alone; I am so alone," pouted Jessica, and still crying, she dropped down on her knees. Rachel slowly walked over to Jessica and gave her a bear hug.

"You will never be alone," whispered Rachel to Jessica. Jessica wrapped her arms around Rachel and cried into her shoulder.

"Let's give them some space," Ally whispered to Lulu and Jane. The three best friends walked toward the playground. They traveled down the long winding road.

"Time to line up!" hollered the teacher.

Ally, Jane and Lulu ran up to the wire fence and sat down in a line.

"Has anyone noticed that there has been a lot of drama the last few days? And that we have not been able to just play basketball for a long time?" asked Lulu.

"True," agreed Ally, but Jane didn't say anything. She had a feeling that the drama had only just begun.

Chapter 25

Billy
The New Kid

Happy to be back at school after his bout with the flu, Billy walked down the hallway watching kids flee from him, but Billy felt better, like nothing that had happened to him in the past could affect him anymore. Ever since Ally joined him at lunch and befriended him, he felt like a spark had been lit in his heart. He now had a reason to look forward to going to school. Billy still might not have a Xbox, but now he had a friend.

Billy headed toward his classroom ready to start the day. The class was expecting a new student to arrive. Billy didn't know what to think about having a new kid in class. In the past, he would usually bully the new person, but now Billy felt like a changed man. He wondered how he would react to someone new.

Billy's class hurried to gather in the classroom. Billy, who was always last in line, finally saw the new kid. Everyone stared at the new kid who was sitting in a chair with his eyes closed, his feet propped up on a desk and earphones in his ears. The new kid was wearing a green t-shirt and shorts. He had blond hair and once he opened his eyes, he revealed startling blue eyes.

"Max," said Ms. Brown, trying to get his attention, but Max just kept on nodding his head to the music.

"Max," repeated Ms. Brown a little bit louder as she put her hands on her hips. She was already starting to lose her patience.

"MAX!" barked Ms. Brown, tired of repeating herself. Max opened his eyes, looked at Ms. Brown and gave her a hard look, which is pretty dangerous to do to a teacher, and even more dangerous to do to Ms. Brown.

"What? You just ruined my jam!" said Max accusingly with a look of disgust plastered on his face.

"Well, I am sorry," said Ms. Brown as her cheeks became red with rage and she put her hands on her hips. Ms. Brown did not look sorry at all.

"Well, you should be," exclaimed Max as he took out his earphones. Billy knew that Max was dangerously close to getting sent to the office.

The rage drained out of Ms. Brown's cheeks as she found compassion for her new student and thought about how it must be hard to move to a new school in the middle of the year.

"Would you like to introduce yourself?" asked Ms. Brown, trying to cool herself down but still keeping her hands on her hips.

"Do I have to?" complained Max as his face scrunched up like he smelled something horrible.

Ms. Brown, who was clearly tired of fighting, gave Max a look that only teachers can do. Max hopped off the chair he was resting on and stood in front of the class.

"Everyone, please go sit at your desks," ordered Ms. Brown with a flick of her hand.

She was clearly not in the best of moods. Everyone hurried to their desks. No one wanted to bother Ms. Brown when she was in a horrible mood.

"My name is Max Reffell. I was forced to leave my awesome school where they let me listen to music," he said as he gave Ms. Brown a hard glare.

"I have no friends and I hate school. I'm from California, and I have been dragged to this stupid state by my mom," said Max in a monotone voice. Max said it as if he were totally bored. He said it like he was a robot without emotions.

Everyone's mouths dropped open because they couldn't believe that someone would be so rude. Ms. Brown's face turned bright red. Everyone knew that Ms. Brown had zero tolerance for rudeness.

"Max, would you please step outside in the hallway with me?" asked Ms. Brown.

If you are in Ms. Brown's class, you know that you never want to step outside in the hallway with her. Billy remembered the times he had had to step outside with Ms. Brown and how horrible it was.

"Sure," said Max, unaware of how badly he was about to get into trouble.

When Billy got in trouble and Ms. Brown asked to speak with him in the hallway, she would give him extra homework for a month, set up a conference with his divorced parents and the principal and make him miss recess for three days. No one wanted to get into trouble when they had Ms. Brown as a teacher, but Max did not know the rules. It only took him three minutes to get in trouble. That was a new world record.

"Please go to your desks, take out your math journal, and do page 143. I will be right back," ordered Ms. Brown as she followed

Max out of the door. No one protested. They hurried to their desks and took out their math journals. As Ms. Brown said, she and Max did not take long, and they returned within a minute.

Billy kept one eye on the door as he scribbled away in his math journal. Astonishment filled Billy's face as Max entered the classroom. He looked completely calm. His face was as blank as a fresh piece of paper. Billy's teacher came into the classroom; Ms. Brown's face was as red as a tomato. Her lips were purple like she had been holding her breath. Ms. Brown was obviously outraged.

Max just sat down in his original seat where the class first saw him. He put in his earphones and started to listen to music while Ms. Brown headed to her desk and picked up the classroom phone. She started to dial a number. Even though Ms. Brown whispered into the phone, Billy could hear what she was saying. Ms. Brown had placed Billy's desk right next to hers, so while Billy worked on his math, he listened to Ms. Brown relay what had happened in the hallway.

Chapter 26

Billy
Going to the Office

"Hello? ... Oh hi, Martha, I would like to send a kid to the office.... No, it's not Billy. It's the new kid, Max.... Well, he is talking rudely to me, is talking back to me and told me to shut up. He just got into class.... Thank you. I will send a student down with Max. Thank you. Bye," whispered Ms. Brown into the phone.

"Billy, will you take Max to the principal's office? You know where it is, right?" asked Ms. Brown.

Of course, you have only sent me there 3 million times, thought Billy as he got up from his desk and closed his math journal.

"Sure," said Billy keeping his side comments to himself.

"Max, Billy's going to take you to the office," said Ms. Brown with her face glued to her computer screen.

Max looked at Ms. Brown for a while as if he couldn't believe it. But then Max took out his earphones and tucked them into his back pocket. Billy walked to the door, grabbed an office pass and held open the door for Max. Max walked through the door that

Billy was holding; Billy didn't get a thank you. Max just stared at his feet as they walked through the hallway.

"So, you came from California?" asked Billy.

"So, you live in Colorado?" asked Max rudely. Billy thought it was not wise to keep talking to Max, so he just walked a little bit faster.

"Hi, Ms. Martha," said Billy sweetly as they walked through the doors that led into the office. Billy looked over at the desk where a woman named Martha was sitting.

"Why, hello, Billy. Would you like me to call Katelyn to come and pick you up here?" asked Ms. Martha smiling, unaware that Billy was not there to see his counselor.

"No, I am here to drop off Max at the principal's office," stated Billy as Ms. Martha's face fell.

"Oh, that's right. Hi, Max, I'm Martha. If you ever need anything, just let me know," Martha said kindly.

"You wouldn't happen to have 1 million dollars in those dirty rags of yours, would you?" Max snapped at her.

Ms. Martha's eyes grew big as eggs, but she quickly responded in a calm manner.

"All right, Billy, would you please take him to the principal's office? You can wait outside for him. They won't be long," muttered Ms. Martha, turning to face her computer again and not taking a second glance at Max.

Billy led Max through the office doors where people were running around with papers flying all over the place. The office was always busy like this. The people in the office were always answering phone calls, filing papers and dealing with angry parents and the kids causing trouble that day.

"Morning, Ms. Sharron," called out Billy to the woman who worked in the front office and who was running across the room while papers were flying out of her arms.

Billy's tension slowly drained out of him as he walked into the classroom. Ms. Brown was at her desk with a line of students next to her waiting for her to check their math. Everyone that was not waiting for Ms. Brown was face-planted in their math journals as the tips of their pencils moved swiftly in the air. During math, people were usually talking and helping each other, but no one dared to talk about anything other than math today. Billy couldn't blame them. Billy moved quickly to his desk and resumed his work. Max headed to his desk, but before he could reach it, Ms. Brown called to him.

Chapter 27

Billy
Math with Max

"Max, there are math journals in the cabinets. We are on page 143. Sondra will show you where," called out Ms. Brown to Max not even looking him in the eyes.

Max stopped suddenly and changed his direction.

Billy watched Sondra get up from her desk and walk to the cabinets as Max followed. Sondra rummaged in the cabinet for a while and then popped out, handing Max the math book. Max said something to Sondra, but Billy couldn't hear. Billy could see the look of offense on her face as she turned and flipped her hair in his face before walking back to her desk. Billy wondered what Max had said to her.

"Billy, please get back to work," ordered Ms. Brown.

Billy dragged his eyes from Max and looked down at his math sheet. Billy flew through the sheets he was supposed to do and then took out his book. Billy was a whiz at math. It was the only thing he was really good at in his opinion.

Billy flipped through the pages of the book and found his mark. He leaned back in his chair and lifted the book toward his face so he could see Max and Ms. Brown. Max was facing his math journal and had his pencil in his hand, but he was not looking at his math book. Billy slowly moved the book that was covering his face and looked down at Max's lap, where his eyes caught a neon green object. It was Max's phone case. Max was playing with his phone. Every once in a while, his eyes looked to his paper and he wrote something down; then he returned his attention to the phone.

Max is cheating! thought Billy as his eyes widened with shock. Billy lowered his book a little to see Ms. Brown. She was too busy to notice Max looking for answers on his smartphone. Billy quickly lifted his book up and darted his eyes back to Max.

He is such a cheater, thought Billy. *What the heck am I supposed to do? I really DO NOT want to get on this guy's nerves, but should I tell Ms. Brown?* Billy debated with himself.

Billy watched Max fly through the questions until he had had enough. Billy quietly placed the math book on his desk. He ripped a piece of paper from his journal and wrote "look at Max's lap. He is cheating!" Then he got up from his desk. He took the long way around the classroom so he did not have to come close to Max. Billy then quickly walked past Ms. Brown's desk and slipped the paper in her inbox. He then rushed back to his seat.

Billy watched as Ms. Brown unfolded the paper and read it. Her eyes darted to Max faster than a bullet. Her eyes got slightly bigger when she saw the green case.

Ms. Brown stood up quickly and took several long strides over to Max. Max saw her coming and quickly turned the phone off and slipped it into his desk. Ms. Brown's eyebrows raised and she placed her hands on her hips.

Oh, Max is so dead, Billy thought as he stifled some laughs.

Max just returned her dead-on stare with an icy gaze.

By now, everyone in the room was holding their breath and watching Ms. Brown and Max. Her hand came off her hip and she held out her hand.

"Oh, Ms. Brown, there is no need. I can walk by myself to the bathroom," Max said coolly as everyone gasped.

Ms. Brown's stare became deadly as she slowly responded, "Give me your phone."

They glared at each other for a long time until Max shoved his hand into his desk and brought out his phone.

"You win this time, you old hag," he said under his breath.

An even bigger gasp filled the room.

"Well, this old hag will be seeing you in detention for a month. I will be phoning your parents today after school. There, we will discuss further punishment. And I will hold on to this phone until they can come and pick it up themselves," she said in a deadly quiet tone. But somehow, everyone in the room heard it.

"Good luck with that one," Max simply uttered.

All of a sudden, against the stillness of the room, Ms. Brown roared, "Everyone, line up for lunch!"

Students shoved their math journals into their desks as fast as lightning. They then grabbed their coats as quickly as thunder. Billy did not bother to grab a coat. When Mr. Wright said that it was going to be nice out, then it was going to be nice out.

Everyone ran to line up. Ms. Brown looked like a commander as she paced along the line glaring at anyone who dared to look her in the eye.

Billy lined up in the back. Even though the front of the line had not yet formed, Billy knew he was going to be the last person in line because he always was...but Billy soon found out that he was wrong.

Chapter 28

Billy

Doctor Daniel

Billy found himself next to Max at the back of the line. Billy did not know what to do, so he acted like nothing was unusual and stepped in front of Max. Billy's class moved through the doorway and Ms. Brown followed Max out of the door. Ms. Brown sped ahead and made her way alongside to the middle part of the line. Suddenly, Billy felt someone step on his heel. Billy looked over his shoulder and saw Max, but Billy just shrugged and kept walking. He didn't want to jump to conclusions. Suddenly, Billy felt a pain deep down in his heel. Billy darted his head back again, but still he saw only Max.

"Are you doing that?" Billy asked Max, but Max didn't say anything so Billy kept walking. Billy felt the pain in his heel again.

That is it! thought Billy. Billy stopped walking and bent down to pretend he was tying his shoe. Billy rolled down his sock; part of his skin was peeling and he noticed his skin was a raw pink. He asked Ms. Brown, "May I go to the nurse's office?"

She said, "Sure, no problem." Flipping her hand in the direction of the office. She obviously wanted to get to her lunch, too.

Billy peeled the sock back so that it did not rub against his injury. Anger bubbled inside of him.

Why did Max do that? Ow, that stings! thought Billy as he walked down to the nurse's office. He had never been there before. Ally would be waiting for him at lunch, but she could wait, he needed a Band-Aid.

Billy turned the corner and walked through the doors into the nurse's office. Billy saw a man sitting in a chair typing at a computer. Against one wall were three rubber beds and against the other wall was a counter covered with cotton swabs, Band-Aids and some unlabeled jars. He also noticed several bottles that looked like they held medicine.

The man turned from the computer screen, looked at Billy and smiled.

"Hi, I am Doctor Daniel, but you can call me Daniel. What can I do for you?" asked Dr. Daniel with a warm smile.

"I need a Band-Aid for my heel," stuttered Billy.

"Totally dude, take a seat," said Dr. Daniel as he stood up and walked to the shelves. Billy shuffled to the rubber bed, sat down and stared off into space.

"So, what did you do? Did you fly off a camel, or did you get bit by a shark?" asked Dr. Daniel, shuffling bottles in the cabinet. A smile filled Billy's face.

"My shoe slipped down and it peeled off my skin," lied Billy. He still didn't know for sure if Max did it on purpose.

"So you didn't battle bears? Or joust with jellyfish?" teased Dr. Daniel. He walked over to Billy, knelt down and unwrapped the Band-Aid.

"Nope." Billy looked at the shelves.

"Why don't you have cabinets?" asked Billy, changing the subject.

"I don't really know; I guess it just makes it easier to get things," answered Dr. Daniel as he cleaned the wound and placed the Band-Aid on Billy's ankle.

"How do you organize your chainsaws and potions?" asked Billy playfully.

"I organize my cooking pots and fish tails by alphabet," replied Dr. Daniel as a warm smile filled his face.

"It looks messy," pointed out Billy, as Dr. Daniel stood up.

"True, it is kind of like my brain. When I am overwhelmed, the shelves are messy. When I feel good and refreshed, then the shelves are organized," said Dr. Daniel.

"That's one way to think about it," exclaimed Billy as he stood up.

"True. Before you leave, I need your name," called out Dr. Daniel as Billy was about to walk out of the nurse's office.

"Billy Bane," replied Billy. He paused in the doorway and looked toward Dr. Daniel.

"Well, goodbye, Billy Bane," said Dr. Daniel.

"Well, goodbye, Doctor Daniel!" said Billy as he walked out the door.

Chapter 29

Billy

It Is Him!

"Hi, Ally!" said Billy. He walked to where she was sitting with two girls.

"Hi! What took you so long? This is Jane and Lulu. Do you mind if they eat lunch with us?" asked Ally. She was excited to finally, officially introduce the three of them!

Jane and Lulu seem pretty nice, so what's the harm? thought Billy.

"Sure, I was at the nurse's office. I needed a Band-Aid," answered Billy as he unpacked his lunch.

"Oh, you met Doctor Daniel? He is pretty cool! When I was throwing up he just stayed next to me and afterward made me laugh like crazy!" exclaimed Lulu as she took a bite out of her sandwich.

"Yeah, he is totally funny," agreed Billy, as he unwrapped his fruit roll-up.

"What did you need a Band-Aid for?" asked Ally. She always knew when he was trying to hide something.

"Oh, part of my ankle's skin came off and it was going to start bleeding," muttered Billy as he watched Ally eat the rest of her granola bar.

"Oh, what did you do to your ankle?" asked Ally curiously.

"My shoe came off, and uh...uh...then it scraped my skin," lied Billy. He stuttered right in the middle of his lie, which made it clear that he was lying. Why was it so hard to lie to Ally and her friends but not Doctor Daniel? Ally and her friends got the hint. They all raised their eyebrows at Billy and he immediately knew that they saw through his lie.

"So you know that Ms. Brown's class got a new kid?" asked Billy as the girls nodded.

"Well, he has a phone. I saw him cheating with it and told Ms. Brown, and when we were walking to lunch, I think Max was purposely stepping on my heel," explained Billy. The girls sat and stared at him.

"Did you say anything to your teacher?" asked Ally quietly. She took a drink from her water bottle.

"No, I just went to the nurse's office after I realized that it might start bleeding. It's no big deal," replied Billy, feeling a little afraid of Max. He finished his sandwich and took out his chocolate bar.

"What's his name?" questioned Jane almost in a whisper.

"Max Reffell, why?" asked Billy as he finished his chocolate bar.

"Is that who I think it is?" questioned Ally addressing Lulu and Jane.

"I don't know," confessed Jane.

"What color hair does he have?" Jane asked Billy, including him in the conversation.

"Max is blond and he has blue eyes," remembered Billy.

"It IS him!" exclaimed Ally.

"How do you know him?" questioned Billy, tired of being in the dark.

"Oh, sorry, he was in the summer camp that we went to. He was in the other group, but we saw him a couple of times. He was really mean," said Ally seeing that Billy did not understand what they were talking about.

"You guys go to the summer camp that school offers?" asked Billy. Only people with low grades went there and Ally and her friends seemed really smart. *And besides Max just moved here so it doesn't make any sense*, Billy thought to himself.

"Nope, the past two years we have gone to a sports camp. It is in California and all three of our families have gone together. They teach us about famous athletes and how to play and perform better in sports," explained Ally.

"Oh, you met him there?" asked Billy.

"Yes, he is really mean but really good at football. I didn't know he moved to Colorado though! He sent two kids home with black eyes last summer. Billy, you better watch your step," warned Jane. She then turned her attention back to eating her candy bar.

"Thanks, that makes me feel a lot better," joked Billy sarcastically.

"Well, maybe he has changed. It has been six months since we've seen him. He could have turned into a better person," comforted Ally.

"Line up," shouted a teacher as everyone cleaned up their trash. Billy saw a group of girls grab their jackets and leave their trash on the tables as they walked to the door, but a teacher caught them.

"Excuse me! You get right back and clean up your trash," called the teacher to the girls as she stepped in their way. *Lunchroom trash is a constant theme here*, mused Ally to herself.

The friends skirted around the teacher, who was now rebuking the girls who had left their trash behind. Ally and her friends shared a smile as they went through the doors and inhaled the fresh air from outside.

"What a nice day," said Jane, taking off her jacket.

"We don't even need our coats," agreed Lulu, removing hers as well.

"Well, I'll see you later," called out Billy. He started to jog ahead.

"Wait!" exclaimed Ally. She grabbed his shoulder and Billy spun his body around to face her.

"Do you want to play basketball with us?" asked Ally.

"Can I do it tomorrow? I need to do something else today," replied Billy. Billy had a plan and it needed to be done today. Playing with Ally and her friends would have to wait, even though he really wanted to play basketball. Ally's face filled with disappointment, but then she replaced it with a smile. "Okay, see you tomorrow," she called out as she followed her friends to the shed.

Chapter 30

Billy
She Did It! No, He Did It!

Billy wanted to see what Max was going to do at recess. Billy didn't see him at lunch today but suspected he would be up to no good. Billy crept behind a thick bush, knelt down and peered through a gap in the bush. He scanned the playground for Max. After a while, everyone was at recess but Billy couldn't find Max.

Where is Max? thought Billy. He was about to give up searching for Max and to go and play basketball with Ally, Jane and Lulu when a shadow appeared on the sidewalk. Next, a figure appeared from around the corner. It was Max!

Max looked around the corner and walked ahead. Then Max went through the trees. Billy got up from the bush and jogged after Max, descending into the trees. Max walked at a steady pace and Billy jumped behind trees and bushes to hide out of sight from Max. The sandy-haired boy paused next to the back of the shed and suddenly turned his head around, looking behind him. Billy was behind a bush peering at Max. Max shrugged his shoulders and kept walking.

That was close. He must have heard me, thought Billy as he followed Max around the shed. Billy peered around the shed and watched as Max jogged over to the monkey bars. Max hopped onto the monkey bars and started to climb. Billy could see a group of boys at the other end of the monkey bars. One boy was sitting on the platform and preparing to dismount, and another boy was standing next to him. Max would have to jump over the first boy or get him to move. Five other boys were standing on the ground talking to one another.

Billy could see Max approaching the platform and it looked like he had no desire to stop. Max moved quickly and was ready to jump onto the platform. There was only a small area for Max to land. Max did not drop from the monkey bars. Instead, Max put his feet on the platform and pushed the two boys who were sitting there.

"Hey," cried the boys.

"What?" asked Max with a smug look on his face.

"You pushed us," exclaimed the boys with angry expressions on their faces.

Billy was now at the other end of the monkey bars, sitting across a bar watching Max and the boys.

This is not going to end well, thought Billy.

"Sorry. I was just swinging and then those girls came over to me and said that I had to push you guys or else they were going to go to the teacher and say I did something to them," Max lied. Max pointed to the girls who were sneaking glances, giggling and smiling at them. The boys started to walk over to the smiley girls, but the boys were not smiling.

"Why did you tell that kid to push us?" asked one of the boys with frustration on his face. He pointed to Max.

"What are you talking about, Alex?" giggled one of the girls.

"You told that guy to push me and Michael," answered Alex. Billy dropped off the bar and rushed to the rock wall, perching on top of it where he could better hear the conversation. Max followed the boys and blended into them, looking as if he were a part of the boys' club.

"No, we did not! We have been here the whole time," argued the girl.

"Don't lie, Cassidy. You are always lying!" said Michael, with a look of annoyance on his face.

"We did not!" exclaimed Cassidy with aggravation.

"Yes, you did!" fired back the boys.

"Did not!" cried the girls.

Billy watched as Max strolled out of the scene. The girls and boys kept bickering and did not realize that the one who started the big fight had disappeared.

"He said you told him to push us," Alex said, pointing to the spot where Max had been.

"Where did he go?" asked the boy as he spun around looking for Max. Billy climbed down from the rock wall and jogged over to where the girls and boys were quarreling.

"Look, the guy that was just here was Max. He pushed you guys off the platform and then blamed it on the girls. The girls never said anything to Max. They never even came close to him," explained Billy. The girls crossed their arms and gave the group of boys a look that said, *I told you so.* The guys, whose cheeks were getting red, started to look sheepish.

"Sorry for blaming you," apologized Alex with a mutter. His face was turned down toward the ground.

"I can't hear you," said Cassidy in a mother's tone.

"We're sorry for blaming you for telling him to push us," repeated Alex.

"We will try to get the whole story before we jump to conclusions next time. Will you forgive us?" added Michael.

"Yes, we will. In the future, please have evidence before you blame someone," replied Cassidy. The girls flicked their hair toward the boys and walked away. Billy watched the boys make ugly faces at the girls' backs and then head back to the monkey bars.

Chapter 31

Billy
Turning New Corners and
Making New Friends

My work here is done, thought Billy. He was done watching Max. He decided that he might as well go play basketball with Ally and her friends, so he headed over to the basketball court.

So Max can be a big bully. He pushes and hurts people and causes trouble, thought Billy as he walked over to the court. *This must be how everyone used to see me, and maybe some still do*, he thought sadly. *I'm glad that's no longer me.*

He saw Ally, Jane and Lulu. Jane was shooting the ball, and Ally and Lulu were in line at the free throw line. Billy approached the girls and saw Ally giving him a warm smile.

"Hey," called Billy, happy to be joining the girls.

"Do you want to play with us now?" asked Lulu.

"Well, since you begged," teased Billy. He got in line behind Lulu. Jane tried to hide giggles as she received the ball from Ally.

"Are we playing knockout?" asked Billy.

"Yep, no one has lost so far," reported Jane as Ally shot the ball and passed it to Jane. Right after she said it, Jane shot the ball and it rolled out of the basket. She was out.

"Fiddlesticks!" cried Jane. She ran to get the ball and passed it to Lulu, who promptly shot it.

"And now I am out," said Lulu, passing the ball to Ally.

"Well, it looks like it is just you and me, hotshot," said Billy to Ally as he shot the ball, which Ally then rebounded.

"Do you want to know the difference between us?" asked Ally as the basketball she shot caught air and smoothly slid into the basket.

"What would that be?" questioned Billy before he turned, shot and scored.

"Well, the difference is that..." Ally paused as she shot the ball, made it and then passed it to Billy. After getting back in line, she finished her thought, "I actually make my shots."

Right as she said it, the ball that Billy shot rolled out of the basket. Billy walked up to Ally with the ball in his hands. For a second, he felt a flicker of anger, but when Ally grinned at him as Jane and Lulu approached, his anger dissipated as quickly as it had come.

"Nice game," said Ally as she high-fived Billy and her friends.

"How did you do that?" asked Billy. It was like she knew when Billy was going to miss his shot.

"Magic," replied Ally with a mysterious face.

"Line up!" yelled a teacher. Billy gave Ally, Jane and Lulu a smile of thanks and headed off toward his line. Ally's and Billy's classrooms lined up at different places, so Billy could not walk with the girls. Billy got in line and watched as all of the kids from the swings jumped off and kids slid down the slides. Billy was about to turn his head, but someone caught his eye. It was Max. He popped out of the long green tube. Billy watched Max head to the back of the line.

No way am I walking with him, thought Billy as he jogged to the front of the line. Billy caught the eyes of some kids and some curious glances and, for the first time in a long time, Billy did not return their glances with a mean face. Billy just smiled at them and continued walking. Billy sat down behind Alex.

"Hey, what's up, Alex?" asked Billy as Alex turned around to face him.

"Nothing, thanks for helping me out with those chicks. Gee, you mess up once and you become the bad guy," answered Alex.

"True," whispered Billy. "I know what you mean."

"What?" asked Alex, unable to hear what Billy had whispered under his breath.

"Nothing," replied Billy quickly.

"Anyway, after you left, we went back to the monkey bars and hung out. The girls came back to us and they kept arguing with us, so we left. The girls followed us, and one of the girls named Alexis asked us who you were and where she could find you. She told us to tell you that it was very kind of you to explain how and what happened and she thought that was very brave of you," explained Alex. Billy's cheeks began to grow very warm.

"Looks like you have an admirer," teased Alex, giving him a friendly push and a grin that filled his entire face.

"Maybe," agreed Billy.

"So you going to ask her out?" asked Alex.

"What? No, dude! We are in fifth grade. We are totally too young for that kind of gross stuff," exclaimed Billy as he and Alex walked side by side on the sidewalk.

"Thank goodness someone else thinks that too!" exclaimed Alex as relief drowned his face. "I thought I was the only one in fifth grade who thinks we are too young for dating. I mean, seriously! Girls are so confusing! One day they like you; the next day they're mad at you. I can't figure them out!" exclaimed Alex. The boys talked until they were almost inside the building and Alex's friends called him to catch up with them.

"Later," whispered Alex before he turned and started to jog ahead.

"See you later," said Billy in a whisper as Alex disappeared around a corner.

It must be nice to have friends you can always hang out with. You would never be the last one picked and you would always have a partner. Your friends would help you with homework, play with you and care about what happens to you, thought Billy as he climbed the stairs up to the second level. *I wish I had friends like that.*

Chapter 32

Billy

Trapped and No Way Out

I t was Spirit Day at school and that meant wild hair styles, crazy socks and a huge dose of fun for most of the kids. But not for Billy.

Alone, Billy ate his lunch silently, nibbling on his sandwich. His mom and dad were fighting again. Lately, it had been more than usual. Last night on their way to Billy's karate performance, they screamed and fought all the way there. When Billy was doing his moves, his parents were outside shouting at each other. He could see them through the karate school's window. When the performance was done, his parents commented on his moves even though they never saw them.

Billy was not in the mood to see kids smiling, laughing and having a great time with their friends today. He didn't even bother to sit with Jane, Lulu or even Ally for lunch. Billy sat alone, by himself, with his thoughts.

Why do my parents have to fight? Is it really worth missing out on your kid's life? thought Billy. He took a sip out of his water bottle.

"Line up!" instructed a teacher. Billy grabbed his lunch box and left his trash on the table.

What is the harm in someone picking up after me? thought Billy as he stormed away through the door. Billy wanted to be alone. He wanted to crawl under a desk and never be seen again. Ally and her friends gave him a look that said, *what are you doing?* Billy didn't care. He just glared at them and stormed out into the hallway.

There was something in Billy's throat and it made him feel like he just wanted to let go and cry his eyes out. He imagined feeling the sobs flow endlessly. He felt a lump in his throat. He wanted to let the rage and despair come rushing out, but he was at school. It was as if he were suffocating in a dark box and everything were swirling around him. The only thing he wanted to do was to cry and let everything out. He didn't want to stay caged in a world that held his hate, rage, devastation and anger, but there was no way he was going to start bawling like a baby, and if he did, *everyone would just laugh at me*, he thought.

Billy felt like he was wearing a sign on his back that told all of his flaws: divorced parents, no friends, bully and loner. He clenched his fists in anger, wanting to hurt the world that had hurt him. His sadness was held back in his eyes, ready to pour out any second. Rage was sharp in his head, repeating words of discouragement.

You were always nothing.

Why should you have to feel miserable while everyone else around you is laughing?

You could never be a real friend. Who would want to become friends with a loser like you?

Billy ran out onto the winding sidewalk and headed toward the trees. When he reached the shelter of the forest, he sank his head to his knees and buried his face in his arms. He sat there waiting for the flood to start as his eyes welled up with tears and he caught his breath. Billy sobbed into himself. The pent up emotions came out and he heaved out his rage, hate, sadness and anger as he repeated in his mind:

I am so alone.
I am so alone.
I hate myself.
I am a horrible person.
I'm not worth anything.

Chapter 33

Ally
Changes

In the spirit of Spirit Day, Ally had her hair pulled into six ponytails randomly spaced across her head and rainbow socks spiraling up her legs. Jane had come to school with neon-colored curlers in her hair but had already taken them out due to their severe itchiness. Her mustache socks were the only remaining sign of her spirit that day. Lulu had colorful feathers in her blond hair that shimmied back and forth as she moved around. As with most days, she had on tennis shoes with no socks as she had forgotten that aspect of Spirit Day. Nonetheless, it had been a fun day for the girls so far, with most of the morning being spent distracted by all the fun hairstyles and silly socks!

Even though Billy was late to join them for lunch, Ally hadn't yet realized that he was backsliding. What she did notice though was a real change in her girlfriends. Jane was more true to herself and did not care about what other people thought, like the other day when Emerson called her dumb even though she was one of the smartest kids in the class. Jane just shrugged and carried on like nothing ever happened. Jane had changed because she had learned that what people think of her does not change how she sees herself as long as she does not believe it.

Lulu was no longer as shy and quiet because she was more open and accepting of herself. When Jane and Ally were about to play basketball and they were both insisting that they were the best, Lulu chimed in. She insisted that she was the better player, finally having some confidence in herself.

Ally's friends were changing and it was a good change. They were easier to be friends with. They no longer cared about what other people thought about them. Now they stayed true to themselves.

Ally was sitting at the lunch table with what felt like new friends, new friends who were enjoying Spirit Day and, at the same time, waiting for Billy to join them. Ally took out her banana and started to nibble on it as Lulu examined her fruit salad and stabbed it with her fork.

"So, did you guys have fun having lunch and playing basketball with Billy yesterday?" asked Ally.

"Yeah, he was totally nice, funny and easy to hang out with," replied Jane. She put a fork full of food in her mouth.

"Totally," agreed Lulu, closing a container that had been full of strawberries a minute ago and tucking it into her lunch box. The feathers in her hair bounced around as she spoke.

"Good, I told you he was nice," reminded Ally. She ripped a chunk off the banana and set down the peel.

"Oh look, here comes Billy," pointed out Lulu. Their heads darted to the entrance.

Ally first saw his red baseball cap and then the rest of him came into view. The three girls watched as Billy slumped into the cafeteria.

That's weird; lately he has seemed really excited and in a good mood for lunch, thought Ally as she took a bite out of her peanut butter and jelly sandwich.

Billy glanced toward the girls. They gave him big smiles and motioned for him to join them, but he quickly turned his head and faced the ground. Ally, Jane and Lulu gave him a look that said, *'what are you doing?'* and then turned their heads back to each other with questioning looks.

"Did he just ignore us?" asked Ally very puzzled.

"Yes, he even gave me a dirty look," added Lulu with shock on her face.

"Did he tell you if there was anything wrong yesterday?" Jane asked Ally.

"Not a word, but he did mention something to me about having his performance thingamabob for karate yesterday," replied Ally. She racked her brain for information.

"Hmmm," sighed Ally, deep in thought. Ally remembered Billy telling her how he had a karate performance coming up, but nothing else sparked Ally's memory. Yesterday, they talked about what kind of sports they liked and who was the greatest dribbler in the world. The girls searched their brains for anything poignant that Billy had said yesterday, but judging by the blank expressions on their faces, nothing sparked their memory either.

"That's weird," declared Lulu with a confused look on her face. The girls ate in silence as they thought about what could be troubling Billy.

"Line up," shouted a teacher, while kids raced to dump their trash and line up to go outside.

"Well, we'll just have to ask him," said Ally. She picked up her trash and walked down by the tables. Lulu and Jane tried to keep up with her. Ally wanted to know why Billy did not eat lunch with them.

What happened? Did something happen at school or at his house? Did we offend him with something we said? I hope he is okay. Wish I knew what was going on, pondered Ally as she dumped her trash.

Jane and Lulu struggled to keep up with her. Lulu's plastic baggie fell on the ground while Jane's half eaten sandwich fell apart in her hands. Ally held back giggles at the sight of her friends. Ally held a spot in line for them as they hurried to catch up. Soon Jane and Lulu dumped their trash and joined Ally in the line of kids bumping each other back and forth.

"I am sure he forgot or something. I mean, we didn't do anything. I just hope he is all right," said Lulu, but she did not sound so confident.

He is upset, but why? Did Max do something to him? Ally's mind went back to the conversation she and Billy had when Ms. Brown and Ms. Nizeley paired them up in class. He had confided in her that his parents fought a lot. *Could something have happened at home?* Ally's thoughts jumbled in her head as she walked outside into a comforting breeze that reassured her a tad bit. She just had to know why Billy was troubled or it would drive her crazy. The girls stopped at the shed. They couldn't see Billy anywhere.

"We should split up. I will search the playground. Jane can check the field and Lulu can check the blacktop and any additional places. How does that sound?" instructed Ally. The girls nodded in agreement and took off to where they had been assigned.

Ally jogged off to the playground. She searched the monkey bars. No Billy. She checked under and on the slides. No Billy. Ally checked all of the swings that had kids in them, but no Billy. Ally knew that Billy had to be here somewhere. *Where is he? Is he upset? Did something happen at home?* Ally searched the entire playground again: under the swings, on the monkey bars, and around the jungle gym. Ally couldn't find Billy. Ally's search felt hopeless. She felt like she was trying to find a needle in a haystack.

I hope that Jane and Lulu are having better luck, thought Ally as she crossed her fingers. When Ally finally declared that the playground had no sign of Billy, she walked to the blacktop. Her eye caught Jane and Lulu sitting at the picnic tables. She walked over to them; then she saw their faces. They had not found Billy either.

"No luck?" asked Ally. She sat down next to Lulu with a defeated look on her face.

"No luck," repeated Lulu with the same look that Ally had.

"Well, where could he possibly be?" asked Ally, feeling wiped out from running around and looking on top of and below things.

"No idea," replied Jane, staring off into the distance while watching a group of boys playing monkey in the middle on the blacktop.

"Me neither. I even asked a couple of kids if they had seen Billy. They said no," reported Lulu.

"Well, we will just have to catch him tomorrow," sighed Ally.

"Line up!" voiced the teacher that they previously had helped in the cafeteria. The girls slouched in defeat as they made their way to the wire fence to line up.

"Don't worry; we will find him tomorrow and ask him what is wrong," comforted Jane as she wrapped her arm around Ally.

"I don't think he is upset with us. I mean, if he is, who cares? It is his problem if he is mad at us beautiful girls," said Lulu confidently, flipping her hair with her hand and batting her eyelashes up and down like a total drama queen.

Jane sent her a quick look that said, *not helping*. But Ally just laughed, *Lulu is right. We can't control if he gets ticked off at us when we haven't done anything wrong. But – I sure hope nothing bad has happened to him or at home.* Ally noticed that she had really come to value Billy's friendship.

Chapter 34

Ally

Reuniting

$\mathcal{A}$lly walked out of the doors with Jane and Lulu next to her, all with backpacks slung across their shoulders. School was finally over for the day and the girls were heading home.

"Finally! Is it just me or was that school day longer than usual?" asked Lulu, taking a deep breath and inhaling the fresh air as the girls walked out onto the sidewalk next to the drop-off point.

"Nope, the seconds became minutes and the minutes became hours at one point today," agreed Jane as she stepped off the curb.

"Totally, the teachers are probably turning back the clocks so we have more time at school," joked Ally. Ally was walking home from school today and Jane and Lulu were going to wait at the drop off area for their parents.

"Hey, I am sorry that we did not find Billy at recess today," said Jane as the girls stopped to chat outside the school.

"Yeah, I am too," agreed Ally. Again, they looked all over the playground, the shed and the field, but Billy was not there. Ally was starting to miss Billy. They gave up trying to find him and played a quick game of basketball. The game ended much faster than it usually did.

"I will see you guys tomorrow," said Ally. She turned and walked down the sidewalk.

"See you tomorrow," called out Lulu, stepping into the parking lot to find her mom.

"Bye," said Jane as she ran to a white car that was waiting for her.

Ally's house was on the other side of the school. As she began to walk home, she heard voices coming from the direction of the playground.

"I know you did it," declared a voice. Ally stopped in her tracks.

"What did I do then?" said a different voice as Ally slightly leaned in.

"I know what you did, you little snitch. You snitched me out to Ms. Brown about me using my phone, you little rat!" exclaimed the first voice.

Ally peeked her head around a corner of the school building, but no one was there so she kept going.

"Well, if I did, then you better find a way to prove it!" said the second voice.

"You dirty scum," the first voice said.

Today is probably the day that I have gone crazy. Either that or my mind is playing tricks on me, Ally thought as she continued to walk on.

"So that must make you even lower than a dirty scum," said a familiar voice.

Ally turned another corner. But this time, she could see someone. Billy was facing a kid with blond hair and a bright yellow shirt.

Oh my gosh, that is Max and Billy, thought Ally and she quickly ducked her head back around the corner so that the boys couldn't see her.

"You did not just call me something lower than a dirty scum," muttered Max with wrath in his eyes.

"Well, if you actually used your brain for once, you would understand that I did just that," replied Billy with rage in his voice.

Billy! Do not antagonize him! That is only going to make the problem worse, thought Ally as she leaned her body against the corner. She took a harder look and could see Max clenching his fists.

This cannot be good, thought Ally. Whenever Max clenched his fists at summer camp, it meant that he was about to hit someone.

Oh, geez! Fighting. Classic male problem-solving skills at their finest, thought Ally.

Her next thought was, *I have to help Billy.* Without even realizing it, she turned the corner and came face to face with the boys.

"Ally?" called the boys tentatively with questioning voices. Max's mouth dropped as he stared at Ally.

"What's going on?" Ally asked Billy. Billy's expression changed from surprise to bitterness. Billy didn't answer the question, and his silence gave Max time to reply for him.

"Why, Ally... How good it is to see you. It has been a long time since that summer camp. I did not know that you went to school here! Billy and I are rehearsing for a play that is coming up. You will have to come watch us. We both got lead parts," lied Max in a happy and perky tone as he tried to hide his momentary surprise. He lied just as he did when he hit someone at camp and then would go and lie to the instructor. Ally could see right through him.

"Nice try, Max. Billy, are you okay?" asked Ally, while giving Max a look.

"Yeah, I'm fine. What are you doing back here?" questioned Billy with a concerned look on his face.

"Aww, how sweet, your girlfriend came to save you. How precious!" teased Max in a mean way. Max's tone had gone from perky to deadly serious, which surprised Ally, but she didn't dwell on it.

"She is not my girlfriend," uttered Billy, looking down at the ground and not meeting Max's eyes.

"Well listen up, Ally! I will fill you in on what is happening here. I was about to teach Billy a lesson. Apparently, his parents never taught him that you do not mess with the toughest kid at school," mocked Max. Billy flinched slightly when Max mentioned the word 'parents'.

Oh great, now Max has another way to hurt Billy, thought Ally as she stood next to Billy.

Ally strategized in her mind. She could see the line of cars coming home from school and work that were waiting in line to get into the neighborhood. Ally's mom was still at work and her grandma was at the zoo with her little brother, who was too young to go to school, so it was fine if Ally came home a couple of minutes late. There could be a problem if Billy's mom was at the drop off zone waiting for Billy. She might get worried if he was not there.

"How are you getting home?" whispered Ally to Billy so that Max could not hear.

"Walking, I live in the neighborhood," whispered Billy in reply.

"Do the lovebirds want to get one last moment together before Billy shows me the proper respect?" mocked Max making goo-goo eyes.

Before Billy could say no, Ally had an idea.

"Yes, would you please go around the corner?" asked Ally.

"I don't know," started Max, but Ally cut in.

"Please? For me?" asked Ally in a girly voice, flashing her eyelashes like a girly girl.

"Well, since I am such a gentleman," replied Max with a deep bow. He then turned and disappeared around the corner. Ally could see her house down the hill.

Puh-lease! He is not a gentleman. Plus, I would never flash my eyelashes, talk in a girly voice and beg – unless it were the only way out, thought Ally. As soon as Max turned the corner, Ally sprang into action.

"What are you...?" asked Billy, but he was cut off by Ally.

"No time to explain, just follow me," Ally said as she grabbed Billy's arm and ran into the trees. Ally and Billy ran through the trees and then a street appeared below their feet. Ally and Billy ran next to Ally's house.

"Thank you," said Billy, out of breath.

"No problem," replied Ally, only slightly out of breath. Her basketball coach made them run like crazy during practice. Who knew that running so much would actually pay off one day?!

Billy turned around and walked down the street, embarrassed.

"Wait!" called Ally as she ran to catch up. "Why didn't you sit with us during lunch and join us for recess?"

Billy didn't say anything and started to walk faster down the street.

"Did Jane, Lulu or I say something that upset you?" asked Ally, but Billy kept walking. She stopped chasing after Billy and stopped in her tracks.

"Is there something going on with your parents?" questioned Ally in a louder voice.

Billy stopped walking but refused to look back. Billy swung his backpack around before grabbing something white from inside and then what looked like a pencil. He paused as he hunched over and then threw something white back at Ally. The white object landed at her feet. It was a piece of paper with a handwritten note that read:

Ally,
Please stop trying to be my friend because it does not matter anymore. Please just let it go.
-Billy

Chapter 35

Ally
Here We Go Again

"You did what yesterday?!!!" asked Jane, unable to hear what Ally was saying. Ally explained how she helped Billy get out of the sticky situation with Max and how she sprinted to her house with Billy, but she did not tell Jane and Lulu about the white piece of paper. She had a feeling that Billy wanted to keep that message private. She had decided yesterday that she would ask him about it later, when it seemed like the right time.

"Wow, Ally! Max was really going to hit Billy?" wondered Lulu aloud in astonishment and fear.

Up to this point, there had been no one in fifth grade who would hit people. There had only been students who left other students out or called each other names and even Billy had mostly threatened harm but rarely hurt anyone physically. Max's approach to bullying was different.

"Yeah, I think so. If I weren't there, Billy would have probably gotten a bloody nose or something," said Ally. She zipped up her lunch box in anticipation of the teacher saying that it was time to line up for recess.

"That's scary. I would have probably turned around and pretended that I didn't see anything," confessed Jane as she closed her water bottle and put it into her lunch box.

"Max kept acting so nice to me, even though he was being really mean to Billy. Max even bowed to me. The silly thing is that he called himself a gentleman and everyone knows that he is not even close to being one," recalled Ally.

"Looks like someone likes you," joked Lulu.

"Yeah, to distract him, I batted my eyelashes and talked like a girly girl," said Ally.

"And it worked?" asked Jane, shocked.

"Yep," answered Ally. She could hear the teacher calling the fifth graders to line up for recess. Ally got up from the lunch table with Jane and Lulu behind her.

"I can't believe that worked! It is so not like you to act like a girly girl!" exclaimed Jane as she walked next to Ally, her lunch box in one hand and her trash in the other.

"Yeah, I could never see that either," agreed Lulu as the best friends lined up for recess.

Everyone was pushing and shoving each other trying to get in front of one another. One of the boys that was behind the girls accidently pushed Ally who, like a domino, toppled over Lulu.

"Hey, stop pushing," said Lulu as she stood up.

"Gee, sorry!" said the boy who had pushed Ally.

Lulu brushed herself off and offered Ally a hand. Ally took her hand and found herself pulled to her feet.

"Come on, hotshots," said Ally. She tugged on Lulu's and Jane's arms and pulled them out of the door and into the hallway. "It's not worth arguing about anyway."

Ally didn't want to see Jane and Lulu erupt in anger. The sooner Ally could get the girls outside, the better.

The girls stepped onto the playground and went straight for the shed to get a basketball. There was no reason to wait for Billy. If he didn't want help, then he was not going to get any.

"Let's take a short cut," said Lulu as she grabbed Jane's and Ally's coat sleeves and steered them through the trees. Ally looked back and could see a group of boys and girls coming out of the doors and breathing in the air with smiles on their faces.

Oh, it must be nice just to hang out with friends and not have a care in the world, thought Ally as the trees started to come into her view. But, honestly, people don't really have "normal" or "perfect" lives. Everyone has something about them or their life that they would like to change.

Ally and her friends came into the clearing and two shadows appeared in Ally's view. Suddenly, Lulu and Jane pulled Ally behind a tree and out of sight.

"Who is that?" asked Jane. She was talking so softly that Ally could barely hear her.

"I don't know," said Ally, straining to listen very closely. At first, Ally couldn't hear anything, but when she listened more closely she could hear voices.

"You are lower than dirt and the sad thing is that you don't even know it," bullied someone with a familiar voice.

"That's Billy," mouthed Ally to her friends.

She was shocked. Wasn't it just the other day that Billy was playing and laughing with her? She wondered what had happened to the sweet boy that she loved hanging out with and that Lulu and Jane had also started to enjoy. Right now, Billy seemed like a totally different person. Ally didn't want to hang out with Billy when he was like this, but at the same time she missed the Billy she knew was the true Billy. She couldn't believe that he was back to bullying kids again.

Ally's face fell as she listened to Billy terrorizing a kid. Ally peeked around the corner as horror washed over her face. Billy was pushing a kid to the ground and he was towering over him. This was not like Billy. In the past, he may have called someone names, but he had never pushed someone before.

"What is he doing?" whispered Lulu.

Lulu and Jane just had to look at Ally's eyes to see her devastation. They understood that Billy was bullying someone.

The nice thing about having Jane and Lulu as friends was that they understood a whole lot just by looking at each other. An understanding would pass through all of them and they would not have to say anything. This was one of those moments.

Here we go again, thought Ally.

"Come on, let's go see what's happening," said Ally. They turned the corner and saw Billy and a kid in fifth grade named Noah, who looked terrified.

"What is going on?" asked Ally as she put her hands on her hips.

Lulu and Jane showed themselves and put their hands on their hips, too. Billy looked slightly surprised, but then his face filled with annoyance.

If Ally had the choice, she would be winning at a game of basketball right about now, but instead she was here solving this frustrating problem.

"And how is this any of your concern?" asked Billy, with his face down and a bitter expression on his face. Ally gave him a look that showed disbelief. Ally couldn't believe this guy! Honestly!

"It is my concern if someone is getting hurt or needs help," replied Ally.

Ally glanced at Noah and could see gratitude wash over his face. Noah swiftly stood up and faced Billy with a look of defiance. Apparently, when girls were around, Noah had to be the big and strong man, but when somebody was picking on him, he couldn't help but be a whimpering and unconfident person.

"Where have I heard that before?" wondered Billy out loud as he gave Ally a hard look. His bitter stare was quickly wiped from his face as Ally returned it with an ice cold expression.

"Why do you bully, Billy? Does it make you feel good?" asked Ally with heat in her voice as Jane and Lulu shot daggers from their eyes. She was not in the mood to be annoyed. There had been enough of this chaos already. All of this drama was beginning to drive her insane.

"Why does it matter to you?" asked Billy, lowering his head to the ground.

"Well, I liked the sweet Billy better than the one I see now. Plus, I thought you were my friend, someone I could count on. But you keep being mean to people. Let me help you!" exclaimed Ally, tired of Billy not being able to see the obvious. She had become his friend and yet he still couldn't see that she was trying to help him.

"Well, I am tired of being the person that everyone feels sorry for. So why don't you just leave me alone? Who wants to be friends with the big bully? And who would ever need help from a girl like you? Why do you care?" asked Billy angrily.

Ally felt a dagger go through her heart. All of this time, she thought she had gotten to know the new, nicer Billy. She ate lunch with him, ignored the people who always stared at her and went through a fight with her friends because of him. Now this was the thanks she got for all of the things she had been put through? No, she was done with this drama.

"Ally?" asked Jane uncertainly, feeling the anger that Ally was building up against Billy. Even Billy sensed the rage that Ally was feeling toward him. Billy's face was a little scared as if he were expecting Ally to blow up in his face.

"Thank you. Bye now," said Noah. He turned and ran toward the trees and vanished from sight.

"Look, Ally," started Billy with a pained expression, but Ally no longer cared.

"You know what? I have gone through a lot to become friends with you. I have had to ignore the rude glances from people when I am around you. I have eaten lunch with you and played basketball with you at recess. I have been through a fight with my best friends, whom I have known since kindergarten, to become friends with a boy who I saw eating lunch alone and who has always been alone. I wanted to be the type of friend that was understanding and tried to be kind to everyone. For you to tell me that all I have been through for you has been a waste is hard. Well, if you do not want a friend or even someone to eat with at lunch, then that's fine by me. I am not spending another second of my time with someone who does not want a friend," said Ally, her voice cracking. She turned her back on Billy and walked away for the first time.

"Ally, wait," started Billy.

"No, Billy. I have been waiting long enough and I am tired of waiting," exclaimed Ally as she walked away. Jane and Lulu gave Billy one last ice steel look and then followed their best friend through the pine trees.

Chapter 36

Ally
I Can Do Better Than That

"Ally? How are you doing? I know that must have been hard," comforted Jane as the girls entered the forest.

"Yeah, I'm not doing so well. I just learned that all of that fighting and drama was for nothing," muttered Ally, taking a seat on a large rock as Lulu and Jane sat on either side of her.

"Well, Billy is a jerk. You have done nothing but be nice to him and be a great friend. If it were up to me, I would have given him a right and a left and a right and a left," said Lulu as she punched the air, pretending Billy was there. Ally held back giggles, but Jane just gave Lulu a look that said, *too much*, and then wrapped her arm around Ally.

"Lulu is right about something; he is a jerk. You have put so much effort into trying to become friends with him. When he said those things, it had to hurt," comforted Jane as Lulu put her arms around Ally, too.

"He should be feeling sorry. He could have had three lovely ladies to be his friends," continued Jane.

"Where are the lovely ladies?" teased Lulu as she looked around among the trees and bushes.

"Ha-ha, unlike you people, I was actually born with grace," teased Jane, getting up from the rock on which Lulu and Ally were sitting.

While Lulu kept an arm around Ally for comfort, Jane walked to the center of the clearing and leaped from the ground like a ballerina. Jane's arms were in an awkward position and her legs were badly angled. She looked like a monkey trying to dance. Jane landed and immediately fell to the ground.

"See, I told you that I was born with grace," said Jane as she brushed the dirt off her jean shorts and flipped her hair with her hand.

Lulu was bursting with giggles and Ally held on to her stomach as she fell off the rock howling with laughter. Ally was so lucky to have such great friends that made her laugh all of the time.

"Well, if that is gracefulness, I can easily beat it!" exclaimed Lulu.

Ally repositioned herself on the rock from which she had fallen. Lulu scooted Jane out of the clearing and bowed her head. Then Lulu sprang to life. She twirled and twisted awkwardly and jumped with her arms in the air. Lulu grabbed Jane's arms and swirled her around in the clearing; then she let go and Jane twirled uncontrollably. Lulu bent down like a frog and leaped into the air, moving her arms into a funky pattern and landing on the ground. She took a bow and gave Jane a funny look.

"Beat that!" said Lulu as she sat down on the rock. Ally had fallen on the ground again. She was on her stomach pounding the ground with her fists, laughing hysterically. Lulu gave a satisfied smile and pointed to Ally.

"See, she is laughing harder than she did with your horrible dance," said Lulu.

Jane gave her a hard look. Lulu and Jane could become actors! They were really good at pretending to have an argument about who could dance most gracefully.

"Okay, you want competition? Then let's dance!" exclaimed Jane.

Ally once again sat on the rock, now beside Lulu, who had a sour look on her face. Her look only made Ally laugh harder. Jane spread her arms out like a bird and flapped them like crazy as if she were flying away from something. Then she turned around with her cheeks puffed like she just ate a ton of marshmallows. Next, she pranced around the clearing while flapping her arms around with her cheeks blown up. Jane made her hand flat and put it in front of her face, moving it up and down. Every time she brought her hand down, she made a different silly face. Jane stopped moving, bowed her head down and flipped her hair.

"And you were worried about me not being able to beat your ridiculous dance! Ha! You should be worried about not being able to beat my astonishing dance!" cried Jane with her head held high as she sat down on the rock.

Ally was laughing so hard her face was pink and she was hugging herself swaying back and forth.

"Can't breathe, can't breathe!" cried Ally after her laughing fit.

Jane smiled at her victory and sighed slightly after her hard work. Jane and Lulu kept Ally laughing through the rest of recess. Ally figured that they were trying to keep her mind off the hurtful things Billy had said to her.

"Time to line up!" shouted a teacher.

Lulu was up next to show off her gracefulness, but she had run out of time.

"This is not over!" said Lulu. She took her two fingers and pointed them at her eyes and then at Jane's eyes.

"I would not think that for a second," replied Jane. She returned Lulu's stare with the same one. Ally wrapped her arms around her best friends and gave them a sideways hug.

"Thank you, guys," Ally said as they walked to the wired fence to line up.

"Anytime," replied Jane with a hint of glee in her voice.

"Yeah, it was fun. Plus, I got to beat Jane at a dance off, so it was a win-win," said Lulu, her joyful face showing only a little bit of tiredness.

"Hold the phone," said Jane, stopping suddenly. The girls stopped, too.

"What?" asked Ally, her face still glowing pink.

"Whoever said that you won?" questioned Jane as she put her hands on her hips and looked at Lulu accusingly.

"Well, I did have the best dance moves, but don't worry, your moves weren't half bad either," replied Lulu, mimicking Ally by putting her hands on her hips too.

Oh great, here we go again! thought Ally as she stood right in the middle of the two girls, looking at each other for answers.

"Hold up, whoever said you had the best dance moves?" asked Jane.

Ally took a glance toward the line. Everyone was almost there. Ally and her friends were just about the only ones who were not in line.

"How about we continue this conversation somewhere else?" asked Ally. She grabbed hold of her friends and started to drag them to the line.

Ally listened to the two girls trying to decide who had the best dance moves, but Ally didn't really pay attention until she got them to the line.

"Ally, what do you think?" asked Lulu.

"Huh, what are we talking about?" asked Ally, who was not paying attention. Lulu rolled her eyes and repeated the question for Ally.

"Who do you think had the best moves?" asked Lulu as she and Jane looked at Ally expectantly.

"Oh. I am not getting into this. This is your problem," answered Ally.

Lulu and Jane just rolled their eyes jokingly and went back to their conversation.

Ally turned her head to the school and could see Ms. Nizeley opening the door. She stepped out and walked over to the line of kids.

Thank you! Jane and Lulu will hopefully stop this debate when we get into class, thought Ally as she watched Ms. Nizeley stop in front of the slithering line that looked like a snake. Ms. Nizeley motioned for them to stand up and then she marched them toward the school building.

Even though Ally's friends had done all they could to cheer her up, she was still bothered by Billy's words.

Who cares if Billy does not want my help, especially after all I have done for him?

Billy can be lonely all he wants.

When he said, 'Who would ever want help from a girl like you?' what was that supposed to mean?

I helped him as much as I could. I thought he was finally able to make friends but, apparently, he's not ready.

I know that it was me that reached out to him, but he made the decision to hang out with my friends and me.

He also made the choice to deny my offer of friendship.

It is his problem, not mine.

I do not care, thought Ally. But somewhere deep inside she knew it wasn't true.

Chapter 37

Billy

The Aftermath of Words Flying and Daggers Wounding

*B*illy had not meant to say that he did not want a friend, but the words had just flown out of his mouth.

The other day he was at his mom's house when his dad came over. They had fought all day and into the night. Billy had to go to bed that night with that racket going on in the background. Unable to sleep, he stayed up most of the night reading a book while listening to his parents argue. Billy had awoken the next morning feeling horrible. He felt like he had slept on a rock that night.

That day was the day he had written that stupid note to Ally and then he had made it worse by saying that he did not want help from a girl like Ally, which was not true! He was just in a really bad mood. That was all. But his big mouth blurted out words he did not mean and now he felt like he was tangled up in a big ball of string. Billy didn't know where the string ended or where it began. Billy was in the middle, unsure of where to turn or where to run.

Now Billy was sitting at the picnic tables alone the day after he had told Ally those things that were not true. Billy's eyes stared at Alex and his friends hanging out at the monkey bars.

"Funny, isn't it?" asked a strange, deep voice as someone sat next to him.

Billy's hatred bubbled up inside of him. It was Max and Billy had had enough of him.

Two days ago, Max had come to him. He had told Billy that he'd heard that he was the meanest kid, and he had asked if Billy wanted to partner up and put kids in their rightful places. Billy had told Max that he would think about his offer but did not make any promises. When Ally found Billy and Max at the back of the school, they were still arguing. Billy had almost denied his offer and that was when Ally showed up. That was why Ally had heard Max calling Billy lower than dirt. Billy had never accepted nor rejected his offer, so Max was there to see what Billy had decided.

He didn't know what to say to Max. Billy wasn't really sure about becoming friends with Max. Max was mean to him and called him rude names and he had also stepped on his foot. Max also might be mad that he and Ally had ditched him. If he became friends with Max, then he might never find a true friend because kids would just become more afraid of him. Billy might never talk to Ally again.

Ally is probably done trying to be friends with me anyway, Billy lamented. He thought about becoming friends with Alex and his group, but Alex might deny his offer of friendship. Billy wondered what would be the best path for him to take. He could take a chance on Alex or even Ally or he could follow Max.

"What's so funny about life?" Billy asked Max, about ready to walk away from him.

"Everything. The way everything is set up. The miracles that happen. The choices we must make. It is all tied to something bigger," he said, looking off into the distance.

"Okay…?" Billy looked at Max as if he was starting to lose it.

Could he possibly have a deeper side to his personality? Before he could ponder that thought for more than a second, Max interrupted.

"I still need a decision. You are either with me or against me," said Max.

"So if I decided to join with you, what would I gain from it?" asked Billy, trying to get the facts straight while stalling for time for the teacher to call them to line up. That delay might give Billy the whole weekend to choose between the three paths.

Max's eyebrows frowned in concentration.

"Well, there are several reasons why you should take my offer," Max went on to explain.

"You will never have kids bothering you because they will be too afraid of you and, of course, me. You will have something to do at recess – putting kids in their rightful place. We both know how hard it is to find someone to hang with and something fun to do at recess. No one will have a chance against us and we will be looked up to as gods. Best of all, you will never sit alone at lunch because this amazing and handsome person will be right next to you," summed up Max as he pointed to himself.

Well, he is humble, thought Billy. He stared at the pavement and began thinking of the pros and cons of partnering up with Max. *It would probably get annoying with Max always talking so highly of himself. Max is right. I would never sit alone and I would have him as a friend. But would Max really be a friend? When he talks, he refers to this offer he has given me as if it is a partnership, not a friendship. All*

I really want is someone to hang out with. Do I want a friendship or a partnership?

"Line up!" shouted a teacher and Billy leaped to his feet and ran to the wired fence. Max got up slowly but did not chase after Billy. He simply stood and walked to the line. Billy waited in line huffing and watching Ally and her friends run to the shed. They put the ball away and uncharacteristically walked to the end of the line, even though the front had not yet formed. Billy suddenly realized if Ally and her friends had sat down in line like they usually did, they would have been right next to him.

Oh, thought Billy as his face filled with disappointment. *They are avoiding me.*

Billy caught Ally's eyes as she headed to the end of the line. He felt dread, confusion and rage coming from her.

Ally is still mad at me, thought Billy.

He knew that he had messed up big time, but how was he supposed to make it up to her? Ms. Brown walked to the front of the line, turned her back to the kids, and kept walking in the opposite direction. This was Ms. Brown's way of motioning for Billy's class to follow her.

The class followed her through the building as Billy thought, *I have to find a way for Ally to forgive me!*

Chapter 38

Billy

What Am I Supposed to Do?

$\mathcal{T}$he following Monday at recess, Billy sat under the slide, hiding from Max. Billy was not scared of him anymore. It was just that Billy wanted more time to sort out his feelings and make a choice. Billy pushed himself against the blue plastic slide. He scrunched his knees against his chest. Grabbing a twig from nearby, Billy poked at the wood chips making a protective circle around him.

Suddenly a face with a bitter expression popped up right in front of him. Billy yelped in surprise.

"Lulu, what are you doing here?" asked Billy as she knelt in front of him.

"What? Is it a crime to sit and talk with you after you ate Ally up and spit her out?" questioned Lulu, clearly still outraged at Billy for the things he had said. Billy couldn't blame her.

"No, but what are you doing here? If you have come here to tell me what a big jerk I am and what a horrible person I am, I already..." said Billy, trying to beat her to the punch, but Lulu interrupted him.

"That too, but something else," said Lulu as she sat down. "Look, after you were such a big jerk and we left, Ally changed. At first, she was really sullen, so we cheered her up, and she laughed like crazy, but that didn't last for long. Now she is downhearted and depressed. She only says things quietly and when she talks, what she says is really short. Jane and I think that she feels like she has failed you and herself. What she said in the trees is true. We did not think becoming friends with you was the wisest idea and we kind of got into a fight about it. She was sure that you only needed a friend and she tried to be one. I hate to break it to you, but you are not really Mr. Popular. People used to talk to us more and play with us at recess, and when you came, that kind of stopped. And for you-" started Lulu, but it was Billy's turn to interrupt.

"Okay, so what do you want me to do? Get on my knees and start begging her to forgive me?" asked Billy.

Lulu gave him a fiery stare that sent his eyes to the ground.

"I am sorry. I had a tough night that night and the words kind of flew out of my mouth. I miss Ally. She is the nicest person and the closest friend I've had in ages. She has always been nice to me and I should have never said those mean things to her," confessed Billy, ashamed.

Lulu's expression softened a little bit toward him.

"It's okay. Ally will probably forgive you. She did for me," said Lulu, remembering their recent spat.

Billy was about to ask what she did to Ally, but he figured it might not be the best idea at the current moment. Lulu still looked upset with him.

"Line up!" yelled the teacher. Kids flew off the swings, jumped off slides (even though they weren't supposed to) and pounded the ground with their feet as they ran to the line.

"You better apologize. We will be at the clearing tomorrow at recess. Be there," said Lulu as she climbed out from under the slide and raced to find her friends. Billy crawled from underneath the slide and walked to the line.

I will be there.

Won't I?

Chapter 39

Ally

Do You Want to Play a Game?

The next day Ally sat at lunch taking little bites from her sandwich as gleeful smiles danced on Lulu's and Jane's faces. But Ally didn't notice their excitement as she looked down and poked at her food in sadness. She felt split. Ally wasn't the kind of girl that lived in drama, but the last few weeks had been full of it. A month ago, the old Ally would have said, "Who cares if people stare at you? Who cares if Billy said some mean things?" but now Ally felt hurt. She couldn't understand why, but she blamed herself. She felt like she was carrying around a 500-pound weight. Lulu and Jane had attempted many times to cheer her up, but only the dance off made her feel better. After the dance off, her smile was wiped clean and she hadn't smiled since.

"Lovely day, isn't it?" asked Lulu, like she was having the best day in the world. Ally glanced at Jane and could see that she shared in Lulu's enthusiasm.

What is going on? wondered Ally. *Jane and Lulu have not been this happy since my fight with Billy. Something is going on. If Jane and Lulu look this happy, then something is going to happen for sure. Plus, Lulu never says that it is a lovely day unless she is super happy.*

"Are you guys okay?" asked Ally, looking at them very suspiciously.

Jane stopped jumping in her seat and Lulu stopped staring off into space dreamily.

"Totally! I feel great!" exclaimed Jane.

"Me, too!" agreed Lulu as she and Jane started bouncing at the same pace.

"So there is nothing going on?" questioned Ally.

Lulu and Jane stopped bouncing at the same time and looked at her as if she had just read the answer to a hard math problem out loud.

"Why do you ask?" questioned Lulu giving Ally a fierce look but still not answering her question.

"You guys are bouncing up and down like you have ants in your pants. And Lulu said 'what a lovely day'—so what is going on?" repeated Ally.

Jane's face filled with realization as she became aware of how bouncy she was being.

"What is wrong with saying that it's a lovely day?" asked Lulu. Ally just gave her a look.

"You never say that unless you are trying to hide something. Like that time in third grade. You said that it was a beautiful day and when we went back to class your mom was there giving us cupcakes for no apparent reason. So spill the beans," explained Ally. She waited for Lulu and Jane to answer her question.

"Line up!" called the teacher as kids grabbed their trays and dumped their trash.

"You'll see," answered Jane quickly as she sped off to dump her trash.

Ally calmly walked behind her friends. She watched Jane and Lulu walk side by side as they discussed something. Every now and then, one of them peered over her shoulder to make sure that Ally was a good distance behind. They didn't want her to hear them talking.

What are they planning? wondered Ally as Jane and Lulu waited in line. Ally dumped her trash in the big trash bin and walked to join her friends. As Ally approached the line, she could hear parts of Jane's and Lulu's planning.

"What if it doesn't work and she gets angry with us?" asked Jane in an almost whisper.

"It has to. Ally won't get angry. She'll know that we tried," finished Lulu as Ally stepped into line with them.

"I won't get angry with what?" questioned Ally with an inquisitive look.

"Nothing!" the two girls replied in unison.

Ally looked at them for more answers, but she couldn't squeeze any more information from them. Her stare was so intense that Jane and Lulu turned their heads toward the ground to avoid her gaze. Ally asked no more questions as they stepped outside.

"Do you want to play a game?" asked Jane quickly.

Ally didn't have time to answer before Jane started to explain the new game.

"Okay, one person closes their eyes and one person leads them to a place. The person who has their eyes closed has to guess where they are. I will be the person who leads. Ally, you can be the one with your eyes closed. Lulu, would you mind waiting a turn?" asked Jane.

"Of course not. Do you mind if I go tell someone something real fast?" asked Lulu.

"That's fine," replied Jane.

"Great, thanks!" said Lulu as she raced away.

Ally turned to Jane and put her hands on her hips and gave Jane a questioning look.

"Really, what is going on?" asked Ally, tired of being left in the dark.

Jane didn't reply. She just turned Ally around.

"Close your eyes," instructed Jane. As Ally followed her instructions, she felt herself being led forward. Ally sensed her feet moving across the uneven ground as branches and leaves brushed against her arms.

Well, I must be in the mini-forest that is near the school, thought Ally as Jane twisted her in a different direction. Jane stopped Ally in her tracks. Ally's head turned when she heard a twig snap to the left of her.

"What was that?" asked Ally, a little alarmed.

"Oh. I… stepped…on a…twig," replied Jane. When she said that, she took multiple pauses as if she were hiding something.

Ally didn't say anything as Jane spun her around three times.

"Why are you spinning me?" asked Ally uneasily.

It was not that she did not trust her friends. It was just that this was all a little weird.

"Oh, I'm spinning you so you don't know what direction you are pointed in," replied Jane as Ally came to a halt.

"Which way is the playground?" asked Jane.

Ally listened to the gentle wind whispering in her ear. Then she heard screams and shrieks and laughter.

"That way," reported Ally, pointing in one direction.

"Correct! Good job!" praised Jane.

"Now, where are we?" questioned Jane.

"We are in the clearing of the forest," said Ally.

"Correct," said a voice. But it was not Jane and it was not Lulu. It was Billy.

When she first heard his voice, all of these emotions came flooding back: sadness, anger, rage, happiness and hopefulness. Ally opened her eyes and in front of her was the person that had hurt her last week. She took a long, hard look at him. Under Billy's eyes were dark circles, as if he hadn't slept in weeks. His eyes were full of sadness and regret. Billy looked a lot like Ally.

"What are you doing here?" croaked Ally, trying to shove her emotions down her throat.

Chapter 40

Ally
The End of the Old

"I have come to apologize," answered Billy.

"Well, why would you apologize to a girl like me?" asked Ally, echoing back the words Billy had thrown at her last week.

Billy looked like he had just been punched in the stomach.

"Look, I know I said some pretty mean things," started Billy, but Lulu cut in.

"You've got that right," muttered Lulu as she stood in the background with Jane. Billy gave Lulu a 'come on, help me out' look and then turned toward Ally.

"As I was saying, I know that I said some really cruel things, but I didn't mean them. You were right about everything. My father has anger management issues. And my parents got a divorce, but they still fight a lot. I have had some really bad nights. There are many nights when my mom and dad scream at each other as I am going to bed. That is why I was so mad and irritable. There are a lot of things in my life that suck. I am really sorry that I took it out on you, Ally. Can you forgive me?" asked Billy, speaking from his heart.

Ally's feelings turned from anger to compassion for Billy. He was being open with her. Ally looked into his eyes. She could see his pain and his sorrow. She could imagine him lying in bed, listening to his parents scream into the night. She could see the regret in his eyes, how he had yearned to say that he was sorry. She could see that he wanted things to be the way they used to be, that he wanted to stop bullying. Ally could see the Billy that she knew before. The sweet, caring and funny Billy that she wanted as a friend. And just like that, Ally's wounds were healed and a smile reappeared on her face.

"Billy, I forgive you. Do you see the difference now between the cruel and the kind Billy? You seemed to feel horrible after you were unkind to me. It feels better to be nice, not mean. Don't you agree? I hope that you always choose to be the kindhearted Billy that I know and think of as a friend," said Ally.

When she had finished, color, hope and bliss flooded into Billy's eyes.

"See, I told you," said Jane to Lulu in the background.

"Thank you, Ally. I do like the compassionate side of me better, and I hope that I choose to be that person too," agreed Billy.

"You may have fixed things with me, but what about those other people you bullied?" asked Ally as Lulu and Jane stood next to her.

Billy inched toward the girls.

"You are right. I have to go apologize to them. Do you want to come with me or do you want to stay here?" asked Billy.

He looked a little uncomfortable when he asked if they wanted to go with him, so Ally guessed he wanted to go alone.

"No, you go ahead. We will stay here," offered Ally.

A grateful smile spread across Billy's face and his shoulders started to relax. He jogged off into the trees and disappeared from Ally's view. Ally turned to her best friends and watched as smiles spread across their faces. Her friends looked happier and Ally felt better, too. All of the regret, anguish and rage had left her, making room for happy memories and joyful times.

"Thank you guys!" exclaimed Ally, pulling them into a big bear hug.

"What did we ever do?" asked Lulu, trying to sound clueless, but she couldn't hide her smile.

"You guys were caught being the best friends in the world!" exclaimed Ally as her friends returned her hug.

"Ah shucks," said Jane, flattered.

"I feel so much better now, like the weight of the world has been lifted off my shoulders," declared Ally as the girls broke away from her hug.

"Good. No offense, but you were a real downer over the past few days. You were just moping around and never completed a sentence," recalled Jane.

"But not anymore!" cried Ally, happily twirling around.

"Line up!" roared a teacher's voice, traveling through the pine trees and echoing into Ally's and her friends' ears.

"Come on, I'll race you there!" called out Jane as she darted out of the trees.

"Right behind you!" said Lulu.

"Hey, no fair! You guys got a head start!" exclaimed Ally, sprinting into the trees.

Chapter 41

Ally
The Start of a New Beginning

Ally and her friends, with one new one, sat at the lunch table eating their food and chatting.

"So, how was basketball practice?" Billy asked before taking a gigantic bite out of his sandwich.

"Not bad. We did the normal. We practiced some plays and, like always, we ran like crazy afterward. I am telling you, one day I am going to come to school with no legs because I left them at practice," replied Ally. She took a sip out of her juice box.

"Totally, the coach always makes us run while our hearts beat right out of our chests," agreed Jane as she stabbed her salad with her fork.

"Even though I don't play basketball or soccer, I still swim on a swim team. My coach makes us swim laps like it is the last time we will ever be swimming. While we swim, he yells at us for motivation, 'Use those arms! You call that swimming? My grandma can swim better than that!' Honestly, he shouts at us like we are deaf," joked Lulu.

Billy, Jane and Ally all laughed.

"Hey, guess what!" Jane exclaimed, suddenly remembering she had big news to share. "Rachel told me this morning that she tried out and will be joining our basketball team! Can you believe it?"

"Oh my gosh! That's great!" cheered Lulu.

"I can't wait to see her at practice next week! That's really good news and a little surprising," added Ally.

"Rachel said she had been wanting to play basketball for a long time and just decided to be true to herself and go for it," explained Jane.

Ally nodded as she thought about how far Rachel had come over the past few weeks. It was so nice to see her happy with Jessica and her old friends while she was also creating new friendships and making choices that felt true for her.

"Line up!" called the teacher. Ally had learned yesterday that the teacher who had cleaned up the lunch trays with them was named Ms. Armstrong. Ally shared a warm smile with her. Ally dumped her trash and noticed Max walking by himself. Billy caught Ally's glance and traced it to Max. He walked over to Max, said something to him and walked away. Max looked back at Billy like he had just slapped him in the face. Billy caught Ally's gaze, gave her a compassionate smile and walked next to her.

"What was that all about?" asked Ally, peering around Billy to get a glance at Max.

"Oh, nothing. It's just that he wanted to combine forces and take over the evil empire," joked Billy as he and Ally walked out of the cafeteria and into the hallway. Ally listened to him as kids' conversations bounced and echoed off the walls around them. Ally could easily tell that he was not telling her everything, but she didn't push him on the topic. She was just elated that their friendship had returned. Plus, there would be plenty of time in the future to ask Billy about what happened between him and Max.

"Hey, you two, what are we playing today?" questioned Lulu. She put her arm around Ally, and Billy made room for her between the two of them.

"I don't know. What do you want to play?" Ally looked across Lulu to ask Billy.

"Don't know," replied Billy as he held open the doors. The girls walked through them and felt the sun beating down on their skin.

"Oh, by the way, were you able to apologize to everyone yesterday?" questioned Ally as Jane joined their line of friends.

"Yep," replied Billy.

"Good," said Jane.

"Do you mind if I do something real fast before we play?" asked Ally.

"Sure, go ahead," answered Lulu.

Ally stopped. Lulu, Jane and Billy kept walking. Billy gave her a questioning look, but Ally just smiled reassuringly. She looked behind her and saw Max walking alone kicking pebbles with his feet. Ally evened up her pace with Max.

"Good afternoon, fine gentleman," greeted Ally happily.

Max just kept on staring at his feet. "What do you want?" he mumbled.

"Oh, my friends and I are about to go play something and I was wondering if you wanted to join us," explained Ally as she walked in pace with Max.

"Why would you invite a handsome man like me to go play with you?" said Max with a hint of curiosity in his voice that was quickly masked with disgust.

"Well, that is for you to decide. You always have a choice," answered Ally. "So...I guess that your answer is a no?"

Max didn't reply.

"Okay then, later!" called Ally as she ran to join her friends. Ally ran to the shed and noticed her friends looking around inside.

"What are you doing?" asked Ally, walking through the doorway.

"We're trying to figure out what we should play," answered Lulu.

"So, we all need to come into the shed to figure that out?" teased Ally. She walked to the wall where hula hoops were hanging with jump ropes beside them.

Billy chuckled.

"Ha-ha. What did you go do?" questioned Billy.

Thankfully, Lulu said something before Ally could answer. "We can play soccer," suggested Lulu as Billy reached out for a soccer ball.

As he lifted the ball out of the basket, a wave of shock came across Billy's face and he had a flashback to his old bullying days. He shuddered as he recalled using this ball to bully kids. He sighed in relief that those days were behind him.

"No, the field is always too crowded," said Billy quickly. He threw the soccer ball back into the bucket as if it were burning his hands.

"Well, we can have a hula hooping contest," said Jane, pointing to the wall full of hula hoops.

"We can do a jump rope contest," suggested Billy as he nodded to the jump ropes.

Ally reached into the ball bucket and her hands found a ball. She pulled the ball out and a grin formed on her face.

"Or you could just get beat at playing knockout!" exclaimed Ally.

She held up the ball so that her friends could see the basketball. Ally's friends shared her smile and they all started to nod. Ally ran out of the shed and everyone raced after her except for Jane who stayed behind to grab the second ball. Ally had sprinted to the free throw line and waited for her friends to line up behind her.

"Are you sure you want to do this?" asked Ally with a smirk.

"Oh yeah, who else is going to beat you badly?" asked Jane as she lined up behind her with the second ball in hand.

"Well, you girls need a big, strong guy like me to keep your craziness under control," joked Billy as he stepped in line behind Jane.

"Well, there is clearly no talent here, so I guess I have to play too," teased Lulu, stepping in behind Billy.

The sun ducked behind a cloud as a cool breeze blew through Ally's hair. She paused and looked around at the close friends she held so dearly. She thought about everything they had learned about each other and about themselves these past few weeks. They had been through so much together – playing endless rematches of knockout, reaching out to make new friends, fighting with each other, making up, and sharing the ups and the downs of real life.

Ally smiled as she watched the scene before her. Lulu was laughing loudly with her head held high as she passed a basketball to Jane, and Billy had turned away slightly to toss a stray soccer ball back to the second graders in the field next to them. When Jane took her shot, the ball glided tauntingly around the rim before falling out, but Jane's grin didn't falter. She simply shrugged as she caught it and waited for Billy's attention.

Yes, Ally and her friends had learned a lot lately. Most importantly, they had learned that they needed to face their fears with courage and honesty.

Letting go of his fears was how Billy became a friend instead of a foe. It was how a fair-haired girl who was always in the shadows stepped into the light. It was how a sports-driven girl learned that words and worries cannot pierce your skin unless you give them the power to do so. And it was how Ally showed the world that we all have bravery inside of us and that it is up to each of us to find the courage to unlock it.

Ally would like to invite you to join the Ally the Brave community - a community committed to ending bullying worldwide.

Sign up at…

allythebrave.com

and receive a free membership including a PDF for kids that introduces:
"The 3 Steps on How to End Bullying"

Made in the USA
Charleston, SC
17 December 2015